MORE BANG FOR YOUR BUCKS

AN INSIDER'S GUIDE
TO BASIC FINANCIAL DECISIONS

THOMAS MARTIN

Visit my website at:

http://YourMoney101.blogspot.com

Wasteland Press
Shelbyville, KY USA
www.wastelandpress.net

More Bang For Your Bucks
An Insider's Guide to Basic Financial Decisions
by Thomas Martin

First Printing – February 2006
ISBN10: 1-60047-005-X
ISBN13: 978-1-60047-005-9

Printed in the U.S.A.

For my Mother and Father

Acknowledgements

I would like to thank the following people for their help and support in making this book possible:

Elizabeth Abbott, Brad Amano, Mylah-Jane Balitao, Scott Bonnel, Kevin Chan, Daniel Dodt, Ed Finegan, Joanne Frank, Sara Franke, Paul Keng, Denise Luckett, Steve Miron, Vicky Olsen, Keith Rosier, Helga Schroder, Neal Steiner, Larry Trotter, Robin Uffer and Ivon Visalli.

A very special thanks to:

Jim and Mary Garlock, the two best friends anyone could ever have.
Mark Taylor, who edited and helped me with ideas when my brain was empty
Susan Richardson, my first editor, who believed in this book even when I didn't.

And to Denise Rosier who said, "You know, you really should write a book."

Table of Contents

Introduction

Growing up, my father was a certified public accountant (CPA), not a fireman as I would have preferred.   Having a dad that was a fireman would have been cool.   Having a dad that was a CPA, was, well, not cool. I really did not know what a CPA did and neither did my friends.   But, after I grew up, finished college and started paying taxes, having a dad that was a CPA was very cool.   He was a tremendous source of information on all things financial.   Not that he knew everything, but at least I could get good basic information before digging deeper into a subject.   He was also probably my first "insider," someone who worked in an industry and could give me honest or "straight" information.

Another advantage of having a father who was a CPA was that there was always someone there to help debunk tax and other financial myths.   I learned quickly that what "everyone" told me could be deducted on your taxes, usually was not true.   Or maybe it was only half true.   Regardless, I knew I needed to be careful and research the validity of advice I received, whether it was from novices or from so-called experts.

After leaving home and starting my own life, my father made the importance of starting an IRA clear to me.   At twenty-one years old, retirement planning seemed to make about as much sense as picking out a cemetery plot. But, Dad persisted and fortunately, I listened.

After entering the real world, I discovered all of the things that I did not know about day-to-day life – from buying furniture to getting a credit card to purchasing my first car.   I was totally unprepared.   My mother always said that she could not understand why schools did not teach classes on basic subjects that we need in daily life.   History, foreign languages, and literature are all noble studies, but unless you are going into education, your first job is going to ask you questions more like, "do you want to participate in the 401(k) plan?" or "do you want to sign up for life insurance?"   Did school prepare you how to manage your finances?   How about writing a resume to even get that first job? According to the Economic Policy Institute, over 40% of individuals from 47 to 64 will be unable to replace even half of their income during retirement. Over 20% of people will retire in poverty. With such grim forecasts, doesn't it make sense that we send our graduates out into the world armed with at least basic financial information?

When I turned thirty, I decided to make a big career change and entered the world of financial planning. I sold mutual funds, life insurance, limited partnerships, and a few other investment products. It was a tremendous learning experience, both positive and negative. I learned after a couple of years that I did not want to stay in this career for the rest of my life. I also learned valuable lessons that have stayed with me and have made my life better.

Because of my past experience in the financial world, I found that people now sought me out for advice. I was the "insider." Since I was not trying to sell a product, yet had worked in the industry, people were open to my opinions. I also learned a lot about the different types of brokers and financial planners that are out there. Many need to be avoided.

I would also look for insiders in other industries. A friend of mine worked selling cars and also worked in the finance office of a dealership. When I went to buy my first car, I met with him and asked two questions, "how do I get a good deal on a car?" and "how do I avoid the pitfalls of the finance office?" He gave me information that everyone should know and you will know too when you read the chapter on Buying a Car.

When I bought my fourth house, I met with a neighbor who owned an escrow company. He gave me advice on everything from selecting a loan agent to tips on ensuring that escrow would close on time.

That is how the idea for this book came into being. We all want "inside information." We want to know, as much as possible, if the information we are receiving is truthful. We want and need to know whether or not someone is taking advantage of us. We need enough information to make the best decisions possible.

Although there are many books available on each subject that I will cover in the following chapters, this book is intended to give the reader a good overview on many topics. I have drawn from lessons learned in my own life and the lives of many of my friends.

2

Like my father, I don't know everything. But I know a lot more now than I did twenty-four years ago when I graduated from college and set out to make my place in the world. Perhaps by my sharing this information your life will become easier too.

Chapter I

Most People Have Made a Serious Commitment to Poverty

The title of this chapter is a saying I made up when I was working as a financial planner. If you do not make a commitment to your own financial security, you are, by default, making a commitment to poverty. Almost no one becomes rich or financially secure by ignoring his financial health. Most people do not win the lottery. Most people do not inherit a fortune. If you take the time, put forth a small amount of effort, if you realize that everything you want isn't everything you need, and finally, if you <u>invest in yourself</u>, you *will* become financially secure.

I considered myself one of the good guys in the financial world. I honestly wanted to do what was best for the client. I tried meeting and talking to people, working to make their situation better. But usually, the best clients were those that already knew something about financial planning. They would listen to me about what types of products were available or how if we moved "this around to there and that to here" they could squeeze out an additional percent or two. Those that did not have money avoided me. It was unfortunate, because the people that I could have helped the most did not want to listen to me. Of course, there was the fear that I was going to rip them off. This fear, by the way, is valid. You should approach every financial decision with caution and seek multiple opinions. But be careful whose opinion you seek.

After becoming a financial planner I met with a long time friend and encouraged him to drop a life insurance policy that he held and invest in the 401(k) plan offered at work. I was not able to sell him anything. After listening to my advice, he called a mutual friend to see what he had to say. The mutual friend told him not to listen to me. If he had called a friend that was successful or rich or in the financial industry, I would have understood. But he chose to call a friend that was barely squeezing out a living and worked in a totally unrelated industry. The sad thing was that I found this to be more the rule than the exception. Although people would never think of asking me how to fix their car, they thought nothing of possibly asking a mechanic what to do about their retirement planning. What is even worse is that most people just ended up doing nothing.

And speaking of cars and mechanics – how many people who own cars have an interest in how to service or maintain their car? Very few. Yet, we know, or had better know, that we need to add gasoline, check the tire pressure, check the oil, and have regular maintenance or the car will stop running. You do not need to work as a mechanic to have a basic and necessary understanding of your car. The same is true of your finances. Over and over I have heard people say that they have no interest in stocks or bonds or mutual funds or retirement planning, so, they just do nothing. Their financial car will eventually stop running and they will simply be stuck by the side of the road hoping that a bus will come along. It won't.

Another woman I met was a secretary for a lawyer. She was 55 years old, lived in a trailer (not a mobile home) with her daughter and granddaughter. She had no financial assets to speak of and no money saved for retirement. Her employer provided no pension plan. When I asked her how she was going to live after retirement, she told me that she did not know. I opened an account for her with $75 and another $75 a month going into a stock mutual fund. In the time she had before retirement, it was not going to amount to much but at least she would have something. After talking to her boss, she called me the next day and canceled the account. I asked her what she would do instead. She said "nothing." The same boss that could not or would not offer her a retirement plan or even offer her alternate advice, told her to cancel the account. I still think of that woman. She would be retiring about now.

I saw far too many people nearing retirement age with little or nothing to show for their years of hard work. There is a tired cliché in the financial industry – "It's not that people plan to fail, they simply fail to plan." It is true though. People do not plan. And in not doing so, they make an extremely serious commitment to poverty.

Financial freedom is available to almost every working American. I hope that by heeding some of the advice I offer on the following pages, you will get there too.

Chapter II

Percentages, Interest Rates And the Time Value of Money

Almost everything financial revolves around percentages, interest rates and time. If you are saving money, high interest rates and time become your friends. If you are borrowing money, they become your enemies and the friends of your lender.

Savings

In saving, compound interest is one of the magical concepts that help you attain your financial goals. With time on your side, you can reach financial independence. The less time you have, the more difficult the task.

In the next chapter I will talk more about long term and retirement savings, but I want you to see how even small changes in time and in interest rates work to your advantage.

As a broker, I would advise people who had little or no savings to start an investment program by putting away just $100 a month. Let's assume my client Bill contributes $100 a month to an investment account. Assuming an 8% return, Bill's account will be worth $1,245 at the end of the first year. At the end of two years, it will be worth $2,593, at the end of five years, $7,348 and at the end of 10 years, $18,295. If this is a retirement account and Bill contributes this same $100 a month for 40 years, the account will be worth almost $350,000 – all for just $100 a month. How much of that $350,000 did Bill contribute? Just $48,000, the remaining $302,000 is earned interest.

Look what happens with higher interest rates or return on investment with that same $100 per month contribution.

	1 year	2 years	5 years	10 years	40 years
8%	$1,245	$2,593	$7,348	$18,295	$349,101
10%	$1,256	$2,645	$7,744	$20,485	$632,408
12%	$1,268	$2,697	$8,167	$23,004	$1,176,477
15%	$1,286	$2,779	$8,857	$27,522	$3,101,605

You can see by this chart that a 2% increase in the rate of return may not make a significant difference in the first or even the second year. But, over longer periods of time it can mean the difference between retiring in a mobile home in the desert or in a condo overlooking the ocean.

This is probably one of the most significant differences in attitude between the "haves" and the "have-nots." When I talked to clients I pointed out that by moving money around they could increase their yield from say 8% to 10%. Their next question would often be "How much more will that make me?" If their account balance was $2,000, it would mean an additional $40 in the first year. Their response? "That hardly seems worth it." Savvy investors realize that by increasing their yield from 8% to 10% they have just increased their return by 25%. True, in the first year it would mean only an additional $40 in interest, but if you constantly look for opportunities to increase your yield, you can see from the above example that over your lifetime, you can become financially secure.

As I write this book, the idea of getting an 8% return on your investment may seem a little outrageous. The stock markets, the bond markets, the money markets and even bank certificates of deposit are paying very low to negative returns. But, these markets will change. When they do, it is important that you constantly seek higher returns on your investments. You will also need to use several types of investments over your lifetime. I will go into this in more detail in Chapter IV on Stocks, Bonds and Mutual Funds.

Debt

Now let's look at the costs of borrowing money and how high interest rates and long payment periods work against you.

Lenders love to entice borrowers with low monthly payments. Those low monthly payments often come with high interest rates and long payment schedules – your two worst enemies. A low monthly payment does not necessarily mean that you are getting a good deal. **In fact, borrowing money based solely on the payment amount is one of the worst financial mistakes you can possibly make**. You must know what pieces of the puzzle make up that payment.

Credit cards are a simple way to get into financial trouble. They are easy money, allowing us to immediately buy those things that we think we simply cannot live without until the future. They have also gotten more people into a financial pit than probably any other financial tool. They definitely have their place. But as a debt instrument, they are terrible. Why? They fall into the "enemy" category I described above – high interest rates with long periods of time to pay.

Credit card interest rates are all over the map. But the real "gotcha" cards carry annual interest rates above 20%. They offer low payments that you will pay on for years if all you pay each month is the minimum. How bad is it? Let's assume you buy a brand new big screen television for $1,800. If you charge it to a credit card with a 20% interest rate, your monthly payment might be only $43. Sound good? Well, remember what I said above – never buy anything based on the payment amount alone. Since credit card companies reset their payment amounts each month based on the balance of the account, I cannot give exact figures on the total cost of your new television. But, if the $1,800 is amortized over 6 years your total cost for that television will be just under $3,100. You could have bought the TV and a $1,300 stereo system for the same amount.

To illustrate further the mistake of purchasing anything based on the payment amount alone let me give you the following example. Using the above big screen TV, let's say the electronics store provides their own financing. You talk to a salesman and he initially offers you a monthly payment of $60. After what you think is some good negotiating, you talk him down to $41 a month. You leave feeling that you got a good deal. But look at the chart below.

Amount Financed	Monthly Payment	Interest Rate	Length of Loan	Total Amount Paid
$1,800	$59.79	12%	3 years	$2,152.29
$1,800	$49.19	14%	4 years	$2,361.01
$1,800	$43.77	16%	5 years	$2,626.35
$1,800	$41.05	18%	6 years	$2,955.89

When you finally make that last payment of $41.05 you will have paid $2,956 on your new TV over six years. That is $1,156 more than the original cost of the TV. Do you still think it was a good deal?

In the chapter on buying a car, I will go into this more thoroughly. Car dealers love to play games with monthly payments.

One myth that seems to persist about borrowing money that I would like to end is that "you pay all the interest first, and then you pay the principal." There is a small element of truth to that statement. But without understanding the facts, this one can hurt you.

The amount you borrow in a loan is called the principal. Amortizing a loan means calculating a fixed monthly payment based on a specified interest rate over a set period of time. For example, if you borrow $25,000 for 10 years at 12% annual interest, your monthly payment will be $358.68. Each month the lender takes the annual interest rate, divides it by twelve (12 months in a year) and multiplies it by the principal balance of the loan. That amount becomes the interest portion of your monthly payment. So, in the first month $250 of your $358.68 payment goes toward interest and the remaining $108.68 goes toward paying down the principal balance. The chart below shows the payment breakdown for the first 6 months of this loan.

Month	Payment	Interest Portion	Amount Toward Principal	Principal Balance
				25,000.00
1	358.68	250.00	108.68	24,891.32
2	358.68	248.91	109.77	24,781.55
3	358.68	247.82	110.86	24,670.69
4	358.68	246.71	111.97	24,558.72
5	358.68	245.59	113.09	24,445.63
6	358.68	244.46	114.22	24,331.41

As you can see, each month the interest portion of the payment decreases as the principal balance of the loan decreases. So, each month a greater and greater portion of the $358.68 goes toward paying down the principal.

The reason I want to make this point clear is some people feel that in the middle of the term of a loan there is no reason to refinance the loan to a lower rate. They think they have already paid the interest portion of the loan and now are simply paying down the principal. You must keep in mind that each month the lender calculates the interest portion of the payment based on the interest rate of the loan against the unpaid principal balance.

I will go into financing and refinancing loans later in this book, but refinancing is seeking a new lender for a new loan and paying off the old loan. This is usually done to lower the interest rate and often the length of the loan, which in turn reduces your cost of money.

Excuse #1: It takes money to make money. Yep, that's right, it does. So when are you going to start your investment program and start making your own money?

OK, what do I do now?

- Start an investment program *today*. How much you contribute is usually less important than *how long* you contribute.
- Always look for higher rates of return on your investments. The greater the yield, the richer you will become.
- Stay out of debt. Only pay for purchases with cash or pay off credit card balances in full at the end of each month
- **Never** buy anything based on the monthly payment alone. Only negotiate the sales price.

Chapter III

Retirement, Long-Term Financial Planning and Financial Independence

I purposely made this one of the first chapters in this book. Retirement planning is *the* most important financial decision you will ever make. Regardless of your goals in life, long-term financial planning is an essential part of those plans. It is probably the only way that almost all working Americans can attain financial independence.

Some people feel that buying a home is the most important investment they will ever make. I absolutely agree that it is extremely important. But with houses and condominiums starting in many areas at $300,000, buying a house may be out of the reach of many Americans.

The keys to long term planning are starting early and being persistent. The amount of money you invest per month is not the major issue. Even $50 a month will buy a level of security that you would never think possible. Of course, the more you invest, the better, but the amount should not be your basis for starting an investment program.

In the last chapter, I showed you how even $100 a month can grow to hundreds of thousands or even millions of dollars over a forty-year period. Let's go back to that same example and see how small monthly investments over a long period of time can change your life.

The two best vehicles for long-term retirement investing are IRA (Individual Retirement Account) and 401(k) plans. An IRA plan is available to all working Americans through banks or investment companies. A 401(k) plan is only available through your employer and may or may not be an option for you. I will go further into these types of plans and their advantages and disadvantages a little later in this chapter.

For this example, I am going to talk about my friend Janet. Janet was not the best student in high school and decided not to go to college. At 18 years of age, Janet entered the work force. She started with a minimum wage job and slowly worked her way into better and better paying positions. But, Janet never became a big wage earner. Her salary topped out at $35,000 a year or about $2,917 a month. But, Janet was lucky enough to have a father who told her over and over to invest in an IRA. Janet listened to her father.

At age 19, Janet started contributing $75 a month into an IRA. Even though her income grew over the years, she never increased her monthly investment. With a standard retirement age of 65, Janet had 46 years to contribute to her IRA.

At age 65, Janet's IRA had earned an average annual percentage rate of 8%. Her account was worth almost $430,000. Janet now took that money and amortized it over the next 20 years. What this means is that, much like a loan, Janet calculated how much she could take out of the account, both principal and earned interest, so that the account would last for 20 years. Assuming Janet gets a 6% annual return on her money, Janet would get a monthly payment of almost $3,100 a month. This is slightly more than Janet was earning on her job.

Of course, the higher the return on Janet's investment, the more comfortable Janet's retirement will be. Using the same numbers, except assuming a 12% annual return prior to Janet turning 65, Janet's monthly retirement check would increase to almost $13,000 a month! All for just a monthly investment of $75.

If Janet can do it, you can do it. But you have to start *now*. **You also cannot view this as a luxury. You must view it as an expense. You must view the contribution to your retirement account as essential as paying your rent and your utility bills.** Many retirement plans allow monthly investments that are automatically deducted from your checking account. Retirement plans through your employer allow deductions directly from your paycheck.

The following example is one often used by financial planners to illustrate the need to start retirement planning early. When I first heard this example, I did not believe it. I had to sit down and do the numbers myself. Bill and Jeff are both 25 years old and plan to retire at age 65. For this example, both Bill and Jeff will earn an annual return on their IRAs of

10% and both will contribute $150 a month to their accounts. Upon retirement, both will earn an annual return of 6% and amortize the account over a 20-year period.

Bill starts contributing to his IRA at age 25. Jeff decides to wait. At age 32, Bill stops contributing and never puts another dollar into his account. Jeff on the other hand, now starts his monthly contributions and continues until he retires at age 65. Who has more money in their account at retirement?

	Total Years	Total Years Contributing to IRA	Total Contributions	Value of Acct at 65	Monthly Ret. Income (at 6%)
Jeff	33	33	$59,400	$463,400	$3,320
Bill	40	7	$12,600	$485,212	$3,476

Jeff contributed almost 5 times the money that Bill contributed and yet Bill's account is worth more than Jeff's account. Bill used time to his advantage.

I want to give a reverse example on the importance of time in meeting your retirement planning goals. Let's say Jeff realizes he will need his IRA account to be worth $500,000 by the time he retires at age 65. Assuming the same 10% return, how much money will Jeff need to contribute monthly to the account to reach his goal?

Age at which Jeff starts contributing to the account	Monthly amount Jeff needs to contribute to reach his goal
20	$48
25	$79
30	$132
35	$221
40	$377
45	$658
50	$1,206
55	$2,441

As you can see, the longer Jeff waits, the more money each month he must contribute. The reality is that he may never be able to contribute the higher amounts. He may not be making enough and there are also limits imposed on retirement accounts as to how much he can contribute in a year. If Jeff starts early, meeting his financial goals is easy. If he waits, it becomes more and more difficult until it is almost impossible.

When I was working as a financial planner I was talking to a young man trying to convince him to start an IRA. He was only 21 years old at the time and did not see the need. I told him if he started immediately, he could possibly be a millionaire by the time he retired. He asked me if I could guarantee that. I said, "No, I cannot guarantee that you will become a millionaire. What I can guarantee though, is if you start this program now, when you are 65 years old, you will say that starting this account was the smartest thing you ever did in your life." I will make that same guarantee to each and every one of you reading this book.

Many years ago I saw an interview with Dr. Jerry Buss, the owner of, among other things, the Los Angeles Lakers basketball team. The reporter asked him what advice he might give to others who would like to be millionaires, like himself. He pointed out that if someone with a moderate income of $35,000 worked one additional eight-hour day a week, took that money and invested it, he too, in time, would be a millionaire. He said that he had worked more than just an additional eight hours a week and therefore had reached his goal more quickly.

Many companies still offer pension or retirement plans. Although these can be excellent additions to your retirement strategy, they can also give you a false sense of security. Most retirement plans require you to be employed with a company for 5 to 10 years before you are vested or before you receive some benefits. They may also require 20 or more years of service before you receive full benefits. Since most Americans change jobs every 3 to 7 years, they may never work at any one place long enough to be vested in a plan. Also, when a company is bought out, years of service are sometimes not honored by the new company or the new company may not even offer a pension plan. Lastly, the benefits people receive from their pensions are often far less than expected. It is not that the company misrepresented the benefits, it is that people failed to fully investigate the plan.

How about Social Security? One thing it absolutely does not do is provide anyone with financial security. Right now the average monthly amount

Social Security provides is about $895 for an individual. That is the average amount. Many people get less. If you retire at age 62 the maximum benefit for an individual is $1,404. Where I live, you can barely afford a one-bedroom apartment for $1,200 a month, much less any other expenses. What is sad is that the amount you and your employer contribute to Social Security over the life of your career could provide a comfortable retirement. Although the original "intent" of Social Security was only to provide a "safety net," we contribute enough to provide a comfortable retirement. It is as if you went into a car dealer, paid for a luxury sedan and were instead presented with an inexpensive compact. Just how bad is it? Assume our friend Janet from above earned $25,000 a year from 1970 to 2003. Janet and her employer would have contributed $3,100 a year into the non-Medicare portion of Social Security. If that money had been invested into an S&P 500 stock index fund which averaged 13.7% for the period 1970 through 1999 and a negative 14.35% for the period 2000 to 2003, her account would be worth $832,349. If she amortized that amount over the next 30 years at a return of 4% her monthly income would be $3,983 or $47,685 a year. Compare that with the $895 a month or $10,740 annually Janet will most likely receive from Social Security. Granted, there is more to Social Security than just a retirement fund. But even if only half went into a private account, it would still give Janet almost $1,100 a month more than she would receive from Social Security.

Do not depend on Social Security. Your financial future is your responsibility.

Retirement Planning – IRA, Roth IRA, 401(k) and 403(b) (TSA) Accounts

Traditional IRA, 401(k) and 403(b) (Tax Sheltered Annuity - TSA) accounts are the three most common types of accounts for retirement planning. There is also a special type of IRA account called a Roth IRA.

With the exception of the Roth IRA, the money you contribute to these accounts is tax deductible and grows tax-deferred. This means you can deduct your contribution to the account from your gross income and you do not have to pay taxes on the growth of the account. When you retire and draw from the account, you will then pay incomes taxes on the amount you withdraw.

A Roth IRA is another form of an individual account. In a Roth IRA, the money you contribute is not tax deductible. The advantage to a Roth IRA is that you do not pay taxes on the growth of the account nor do you pay taxes when you withdraw from it.

A traditional Individual Retirement Account (IRA) is available to all working Americans. Currently, an individual, not covered by any other retirement plan (e.g. 401(k) or 403(b)) can contribute up to $3,000 a year and deduct the contribution. You may contribute to the account annually, bi-annually, quarterly, monthly, etc. Just be sure that you do not exceed the annual amount allowed. The annual limit to IRA contributions does change so you want to be aware of the current maximum. IRAs can also be used to accept rollover money from other retirement plans. I will discuss this concept later in this chapter.

Both regular IRA and Roth IRA funds may be invested in a variety of accounts. The easiest is to simply go to your bank and open an account. Your bank will generally suggest the money be placed into a certificate of deposit (CD). You can also go to a brokerage house, such as Charles Schwab, Ameritrade, E-Trade or Merrill Lynch and open an account with them. A brokerage house offers a much wider selection of investment options. Usually they will suggest investing the money in one or more mutual funds. Banks often have investment counselors in their offices that can help you with these types of investments as well. You can also use insurance products, but I do not recommend them. The chapter on Life Insurance and Annuities explains this in more detail.

Tax-sheltered Annuity (TSA) or 403(b) accounts are available only to teachers and employees of non-profit organizations. These accounts are not set up through the school or non-profit organization. Instead you meet with representatives of various insurance or investment companies and they set up the annuity. Your contribution is usually deducted directly from your paycheck and deposited into the account. If this is the only plan available to you, I do recommend taking advantage of it. But please read more on this subject in the chapter on Life Insurance and Annuities. There are many caveats of which you need to be aware. If you do participate in a 403(b) program, you may be able to roll existing annuities into an IRA. Depending upon the surrender fees, this could be a tremendous benefit.

A 401(k) account is only offered through your employer. You usually have the opportunity to sign up for the plan when you are hired or sometime during the year. If a 401(k) plan is offered to you by your employer (or your spouse's employer) you may still contribute to an IRA but your contributions will most likely not be tax-deductible because of the laws governing retirement accounts. A 401(k) is usually the best option available for retirement planning. The maximum amount that can be contributed to a 401(k) plan is usually much higher than an individual retirement account. The current annual limit is $12,000 but that amount can be less depending on the participants in the plan. It can also be more, depending on your age. Check with your employer for the limits on the 401(k) plan available to you.

When establishing a 401(k) plan, you will be given investment options. In most cases, the plan provider will offer choices of several mutual funds. They will often include different types of stock funds, bond funds and usually some sort of a money market or guaranteed interest earning fund. You can distribute your contributions between one or more of these funds. I will go into more detail on these types of investments in the chapter on Stocks, Bonds and Mutual Funds.

Your 401(k) account may also offer the purchase of company stock. Long-term employees of Microsoft and Wal-Mart have reaped the benefits of such a program. Although this option may sound tempting, I would recommend that no more than 10% of your retirement account be placed in any one company, even your own. Employees of Enron and Global Crossings learned this painful lesson when their investments became worthless or almost worthless. Keep your funds diversified.

One of the greatest benefits of 401(k) accounts is employers will often match a certain percentage of your contribution. For example, if you contribute 2% of your gross salary, your employer may contribute another 2%. Does this sound like a good deal? You bet it is. Let's look at how easy it is to reach financial security using a 401(k) account.

Our friend Bill makes $24,000 a year or $2,000 a month. His employer offers a 401(k) plan which matches the first 2% of Bill's contribution. Bill decides that he will start the plan with 2% of his salary. This means that Bill will be contributing $40 a month to his account. But, since this amount is pre-tax, or taken out of his pay before income taxes are calculated, the net change to his paycheck might only be $30 a month, depending on his tax rate. Bill's employer then matches the 2% by contributing another $40 into the account. So, for what Bill sees on his check as only a $30 a month change in his net pay, he is actually placing $40 into his account and his employer is placing another $40 for a monthly total of $80.   A year later, Bill gets a raise and wisely increases his contribution to 4%.   Before he gets used to the additional income, he bumps up his contribution amount.

Rolling Over Your 401(k) to an IRA

When you leave a company where you have participated in a 401(k) plan you are usually given the option of leaving the money in the account or rolling it over into another qualified plan, such as an IRA.   You can withdraw the money, but you will be required to pay taxes and possibly penalties on the withdrawal.

A rollover is simply moving money from one retirement account (qualified plan) into another. In doing so, you avoid paying taxes or penalties.   I strongly recommend that any time you leave a company where you have established a 401(k) account, you roll the money over into your own IRA account.   If you have not established an IRA, go to your bank or brokerage house and tell them that you want to open a rollover IRA account.   They will help you to direct the money from the 401(k) plan to your new account. **Be sure to keep a copy of the statement showing the money that was deposited into the IRA.**   It is not unusual for the IRS to request a copy of this statement to ensure the money was actually rolled over into another qualified retirement plan.

There are four reasons why I recommend moving your money from a 401(k) plan to your own IRA after leaving a company.

1. 401(k) plans have a trustee that oversees the accounts. These trustees charge fees for their services which are passed on to the account holders. These fees usually do not apply to IRA accounts.

2. I feel that it is better to have your money in one place if possible. If you change employers every two years and establish a 401(k) account with each of them, at the end of 10 years, you will be overseeing 5 different accounts. If the first four are rolled over into an IRA, you will simply have your principal IRA account and the 401(k) account with your current employer.

3. Your investment options in a 401(k) plan are limited. Usually the plan will make available 10 to 20 different funds in which you can invest. If you open an IRA account with a brokerage house, this

expands to several hundred. You can also take advantage of other types of investments usually not available through any 401(k) plan such as individual stocks and a much wider range of mutual funds.

4. Although this is extremely rare, it has happened that some employers have absconded with the money that employees thought they were placing into their 401(k) accounts. I would not lose any sleep over this, but I just feel better having it all close to home.

If you are self-employed, there are additional types of retirement accounts (such as SEP-IRA and Keogh accounts) available to you that may offer more flexibility than those described above. When speaking to your broker or investment counselor, be sure to mention that you are in business for yourself and ask about what programs might benefit your situation.

Withdrawals from retirement plans cannot begin until age 59½. If you withdraw money prior to that time, you may be subject to penalties and taxes. There are programs by which you can withdraw money to purchase a home or to use for education. In these cases the money may not be subject to penalties. In my opinion, this should never be done except in extreme circumstances. Once you withdraw or, in cases of 401(k) programs, borrow from the plan, you are jeopardizing your retirement program. I am strongly in favor of home purchases. But, as I said at the beginning of this chapter, your long-term retirement planning is the most important part of reaching financial security. Do not take chances with this fund.

If you take my advice and begin contributing to a retirement plan early in your life, you can see that you can reach financial security by contributing even $100 a month. I have met a couple of smart young professionals that immediately began contributing 10% to 14% of their income into their 401(k) programs. My advice to them was to reduce their contribution to 6% and take the remaining amount and place it into a non-retirement investment plan that can be accessed at any time during their lives. There are two reasons for this.

1. Your retirement fund is only available to you after age 59½. If you make large contributions to your account starting at age 22 and also enjoy good returns on your investment, it is possible for you to have enough money saved to retire at age 50. But, if everything is in your retirement account, you will still need to wait another 10 years. So, this leads to my second point.

2. By opening and contributing to a savings account or what is called a "cash" or "open" account through an investment company, you can have money available to you when you need it. The money from this medium-term investment strategy can be used for a home purchase or could potentially allow you to retire early. This money can bridge the gap, using my prior example, from age 50 to 59½.

All working Americans have the opportunity for financial security. If you start early, the cost to you is small. Dinner and a movie for two can easily cost $50. Is forgoing that once a month really that much of a sacrifice?

Excuse #2: "I don't have enough money left over at the end of the month to start an investment program." You don't if you do not make it a priority. Americans tend to live up to or past their income level. It does not seem to matter if someone makes $10,000 or $100,000 per year, I keep hearing this same excuse. If your income was cut 10% because of a job change, you would adapt, because you would have to adapt. If you were offered a new job that over the next 10 years would triple your annual income, but for the first year, you would have to take a pay cut of 15%, would you do it? If you could see past the next month or two, you would jump at the chance. All you need to do is to start taking a small amount of your monthly income and begin an investment program. As I said earlier, you must view this as a monthly expense, much as you would view the cost of rent or the cost of food. The next time you get an increase in your monthly income, simply take half of that amount and begin an investment program. Keep doing that each time you get a raise and you will reach financial independence before you know it.

Regardless of what you make now, if you honestly think you cannot afford to put away even $100 a month, how are you going to afford living on the $1,400 a month or less that you will get from Social Security?

OK, What do I do now?

- Immediately open and begin contributing to a 401(k) plan at work or an IRA if a 401(k) is not available to you. If you are a teacher, open a TSA (403(b)) plan.
- View long-term financial planning as a monthly expense, not a luxury.
- When you change employers, roll your 401(k) money into an IRA

Chapter IV

Stocks, Bonds and Mutual Funds

The topic of this chapter is the entire subject of many books. If you are interested in learning more about investing in the stock market directly, please read Peter Lynch's book, *One Up On Wall Street*. It is well written, easy to follow and gives good, solid advice.

What I want to do is give you a basic overview of different types of investments. In starting a retirement plan, or a medium or long-term investment program, you will need to make investment selections. I want you to have enough information to make informed decisions. For the average American, the easiest way to invest in different markets is through mutual funds. Stocks, bonds and money market instruments are the most common components of mutual funds. This short introduction to these types of investments will assist you in making good investment decisions.

Stocks, Stock Markets and Stock Indexes

By buying stock you are actually becoming a partial owner in a company. Stock is purchased in units called shares. Each share represents a small percentage of ownership in the company. Shares of stock are purchased through various exchanges such as the New York Stock Exchange (NYSE) and the American Stock Exchange (AMEX). These exchanges are markets where buyers and sellers come together to trade ownership of stock. Trades in these exchanges are executed by brokerage firms such as Charles Schwab and Merrill Lynch.

There are two basic reasons to buy stock. The first is growth. You invest in a small company because you expect it to get bigger and bigger and make more and more money. As it grows, the company becomes more valuable and so, the value of your shares of stock also grows. The second reason is for dividends. Large companies, such as IBM, do not have the potential for growth that small companies might have. But, large companies are much more likely to be profitable. These companies usually take a portion of their profits and pay it out to their shareholders. The percentage calculated by dividing the annual dollar amount of the dividend by the current share price is the yield of that stock. In some cases, such as utility companies, there is almost no potential for growth and the stock in those companies is purchased almost solely for the dividends.

Of the investments I will discuss in this book, stocks give you the *opportunity* for the greatest return on your investment.

When you hear the stock markets discussed on the news, they are constantly referring to different stock indexes such as the Dow Jones Industrial Average (DJIA), the S&P 500 (SPX), the NASDAQ (NDX), and various other indexes. An index is simply a tool used by the exchanges to indicate the general trend of the broad market or within certain sectors of the market. The most well known index is the Dow Jones Industrial Average. It is comprised of 30 large companies that the Dow Jones company sees as representing their specific industries. For example, the computer industry is represented in the DJIA by IBM and Microsoft. The auto industry is represented by General Motors. Other well known companies in the DJIA are Wal-Mart, Exxon Mobile, and J.P. Morgan Chase. The stock prices of each of these companies are used to create the Dow Jones Industrial Average. The Dow Jones company also provides indexes in specific sectors such as the transportation and the health care industries.

The Standard and Poor's 500 stock index (S&P 500) is another often quoted index. It is an index of the 500 top U.S. companies. Because it includes 500 companies in its index versus the Dow Jones Industrial index of 30 companies, it gives a better indication of the movements in the broader market.

Bonds

Bonds are debt instruments issued by corporations and government agencies. More simply, they are ways for companies and governments to borrow money. Bonds are usually purchased in increments of $10,000. They have an interest rate fixed for the life of the bond and usually pay interest quarterly. The length of maturity on bonds can be 5-years, 10-years, 20-years or even 30-years. In general, the longer the maturity of the bond, the lower the interest rate paid by the borrower.

Bonds are rated as to their safety by several independent rating companies such as Moody's and Standard and Poor's. The lower the rating, the higher the yield and the higher the risk. Whether you are buying bonds directly or in a mutual fund, be sure to investigate the bond's rating before investing.

For example, XYZ Corporation wants to raise money to expand its operation. XYZ will need $100 million in financing. The company can go to a bank and borrow the money or it can borrow from the public by issuing bonds. The interest rate paid on the bonds is determined by the credit worthiness of the company. The safer or more stable the company, the lower the interest rate to be paid. Let's say you decide to buy one of these bonds, which, in our case, is a 10-year bond. You give XYZ corporation $10,000 and you receive a bond. Attached to the bond are coupons. These coupons are used to collect the interest on the bond usually every three months or quarterly. At the end of the 10 years, the bond itself is redeemed for the original $10,000 investment.

As interest rates change, the value of your bond will also change. Bonds can be traded in markets much like stocks are traded. You do not need to hold the bond until its maturity. You can sell the bond at any time on the open market. But, depending on the length of time to maturity of your bond and the current interest rates, you may get your original $10,000 for the bond or you may get more or less. As interest rates rise, the value of your bond decreases, as interest rates decline, the value of your bond increases. As your bond gets closer and closer to its maturity date, it returns to the original value of $10,000.

Let's say that you buy a 10-year bond for $10,000 with an interest rate of 3%. One year later, you decide to sell the bond. At that time, interest rates have risen and bonds now have a 4% interest rate. Why would anyone buy your bond with a three percent rate when they could now buy a bond with a four percent rate? The only reason is that you now "discount" your bond, or reduce the face value from $10,000 to a lower price that yields the purchaser of your bond the current rate of 4%. Of course, the reverse is also true. If you own a bond with a yield of 10% and interest rates have dropped to 8%, you will be able to sell your bond for more than the face value of $10,000. Regardless of what you paid for your bond, when it comes time to redeem it at the end of 10 years, you will still get the original $10,000.

Money Markets

Money market instruments consist of a variety of short-term debt notes. Since these notes have a very short maturity date, their value remains constant. Their return also varies according to current market conditions. They are liquid, meaning you can easily move money in and out of money market notes. Money market accounts in banks or in mutual funds are a tremendous tool you can use in investing. Their use will become clearer as I talk about mutual funds.

Mutual Funds

What is a mutual fund? Let me use the following example. Let's say that our friend Bill has an uncle who is quite wealthy. Uncle Jim seems to have the Midas touch, whatever he does he makes money. Bill does not know much about investing and would like the help of his uncle. As Bill discusses this with his wife and other family members, they also would like the help of Uncle Jim. But Uncle Jim is a busy man, he does not have the time to give weekly or monthly investment updates to each family member. Instead, Uncle Jim suggests that each family member deposits $5,000 into a type of joint account. Each share of the account is worth $1. So Bill starts out with 5,000 shares in the account. Uncle Jim has investment control of the account and invests the money as he sees best. As the value of the account grows, the share value also grows. As compensation for his efforts, Uncle Jim is paid a small percentage of the account each year.

Bill and the other members of his family have allowed a professional to oversee their investments. In doing so, Bill does not have to track each stock or bond in his account. Uncle Jim takes care of that for him. Uncle Jim might invest in stocks, bonds, money market instruments, real estate, gold, or other investment options. Later, Bill decides he needs a portion of the money in the account to buy a house. Uncle Jim sells enough of the investments in the account to redeem Bill's shares.

That is basically how a mutual fund works. People buy shares in a fund and the money is then professionally managed and invested. The mutual fund company receives compensation from a small percentage of the fund's total value. Usually, a fund has some sort of investment objective. It may invest only in stocks, only in government bonds, only in corporate bonds, only in certain sectors of stocks, such as technology, or it may diversify across several types of investments. Because mutual funds are professionally managed and are able to diversify across many stocks or bonds, they usually represent a less risky form of investing than if you invested the money yourself.

When you open a 401(k) account with your employer, you will be given several investment options. The plan administrator usually selects 10 to 20 different mutual funds to be part of the plan. When you start the account you will be asked not only how much money you want deducted from your salary to go into the plan but also how you want that money invested. Mutual funds are most commonly broken down into the following categories:

Stock (Equity) Funds
   Large Capital (Large or Big Cap) – These funds invest in large companies such as IBM and General Motors. They have less potential for growth than medium and small capital funds, but are usually more stable. They often derive some of their return from dividends paid by the stocks in the fund. Often these companies have a capitalization or worth of greater than $1 billion.
   Medium Capital (Medium or Mid-Cap) – These funds invest in medium size companies often with a capitalization or worth of greater than $250 million. Because of this, they have a greater opportunity for growth than large capital funds. They are also subject to greater price fluctuations and present a slightly greater risk than the large capital funds.
   Small Capital (Small Cap) – Like the name implies, these funds invest in smaller companies, often with a capitalization of greater than $50 million. They provide the greatest opportunity for growth and return on your investment. They also present the greatest risk level of these three types of stock mutual funds.
   Index Funds – Index funds invest in the same mix of stocks that comprise the underlying stock index. For example, the most common stock index funds are S&P 500 funds. Your money is invested across the same 500 companies that are represented in the S&P 500 stock index. As the stocks that comprise the index change, so do the holdings of this type of mutual fund. The management fees for these funds are usually the lowest. The majority of managed stock mutual funds have historically been unable to beat the S&P 500 index. This is almost always a good investment decision for long-term investing.
   Income Stock Funds (Equity Income) – These funds invest in stocks with good yields. In other words, stocks that pay dividends. They

are selected less for their growth potential and more for their income potential.

International Funds – These funds invest in stocks from other countries. In general, I do not recommend this type of investment for retirement planning. These funds can be affected by fluctuations in the currency markets.

Sector Funds – These funds will not likely appear in the options available in a 401(k) account, but are available through brokerage firms for an IRA. Sector funds invest in stocks of a specific industry such as health care or technology. Since they are less diversified, they are considered to carry more risk.

Bond Funds

Government – These funds hold a variety of government issued bonds and other debt instruments. They usually are the safest of the bond funds but often have the lowest yields. Do not be misled into thinking that because these are U.S. Government bonds that the principal is guaranteed. Like any bond, the underlying bond value can fluctuate as interest rates rise and fall.

High Grade Corporate – These are the best of the corporate bond funds.

High Yield Corporate – High Yield can also mean "junk." These funds are comprised of low grade and no grade bonds. The companies that issue these bonds are often of higher risk so the yields are also higher.

Tax-Free – Tax-free bonds are usually issued by municipalities and the interest paid is exempt from federal taxes and in some cases state taxes. The yields on tax-free bonds are usually much lower than other types of bonds. Because of this, they are not appropriate for retirement accounts. Outside of retirement accounts, they are usually only of value to people in the highest tax bracket. You are usually better off investing in higher yielding bonds and paying the required tax.

Money Market or Fixed Funds (Stable Value)

These funds are comprised of many types of short-term debt instruments as described above. The advantage of money market funds is that your principal amount is not subject to price fluctuations. The share price is almost always $1 and remains $1. The interest rate or yield paid on the account fluctuates as interest rates change. In general, these funds are good places to park your money while moving from one investment to another or when you are looking for a "safe haven." In times when interest rates are high, these funds can also be used for a good return on your money.

Investment Allocation

Within your retirement account you will usually be able to select one or more funds in which your money is to be invested. You can put all of the money into one fund or break it up among several funds. It is usually best to divide the money between two or three funds.

The funds you select depend on your financial objective or on the amount of time you have until you retire.

Five or more years until retirement – It is usually best to place the majority of the money into stock funds. I recommend that 80% of the money be split between two or more stock funds and the remaining 20% invested in a bond fund. I would select an Index Fund (preferably an S&P500 Index Fund) and a Small or Mid-Cap stock fund. The bond fund should be either a government fund or a high-grade corporate bond fund.

Five or less years until retirement – At this point, you need to start protecting your principal. Income-type stock funds now become more attractive. I recommend moving your stock fund holdings into index, large-cap funds and stock income funds. Reduce the amount held in stock funds to 70% and increase your bond fund holdings to 30%.

During retirement – At this point, you will probably be seeking income from your retirement account. But, your account is also going to need to grow to provide income for the next twenty or more years. I recommend placing the majority of your account in income producing funds such as bonds, money markets and stock income funds. If possible, I suggest leaving 20% of the account in a mid-cap or large-cap stock fund for at least the first five to ten years of your retirement.

The above suggestions have worked well over the last twenty to twenty-five years. But, should interest rates rise and you are able to get over 8% on your money in certificates of deposit or in money market accounts you probably should look at re-allocating your investments. As rates are rising, money market accounts will usually give the best return. If you are able to see when rates have peaked and are beginning to fall, then locking in the rate in the form of a long term bond or a certificate of deposit could be a good move.

There are many other types of investments available, although not usually through retirement accounts. As I mentioned before, the purpose of this chapter is not to turn you into a professional trader. On the other hand, I do want to cover two other types of investments. These investments are too often inappropriately sold to people and the risks and limitations are not fully explained.

Limited Partnerships

A limited partnership is a form of business in which there is a general partner, who organizes and manages the partnership, and limited partners who contribute capital but have limited liability. Limited Partnerships often invest in real estate projects and oil or gas exploration. An advantage of limited partnerships is that tax benefits, such as depreciation, are passed down to the limited partners. The biggest disadvantage is there is no secondary market for limited partnerships. This means that once you invest in a limited partnership, there may not be a market where you can sell the partnership and get your money out. Limited Partnerships usually have a life of 10 years, although some may be much longer. They are not appropriate for the average investor. Also, many, such as oil and gas exploration, involve considerable risk. I also saw limited partnerships that seemed to be selling tax deductions rather than a good underlying investment. Limited partnership sales mean good commissions for your broker. He or she may be motivated to get you into one even though it is not an appropriate investment for you. Be careful before investing any money into a limited partnership. Get the prospectus from your broker and discuss it with several knowledgeable people before investing.

Options and Futures

Options and Futures markets are basically ways in which you can "bet" on the future price of a stock, commodity or index. There are promises of great returns from brokers that deal specifically with these types of investments. Do not believe them. Yes, there is the potential for gain, but then, there is also the potential for huge returns from playing the lottery. Both of them are risky investments.

There is definitely a place for these types of investments, but I know few people that understand how to use them to their advantage. When viewed as a "get rich quick scheme," you are likely to be on the losing end.

Financial Planners and Advisers

There are a lot of people out there that call themselves "financial planners." Most are little more than salespeople for insurance or small financial services companies. These companies ram them through a course to get their licenses, tell them why their products are best, and then send them out to hit up their friends and families. How do I know? Because that is how I got started. I was originally armed with just enough information to make it sound like I knew what I was talking about. I did know more than the average person, but my information was skewed to the advantage of the company for which I was working. But I caught on; I changed companies and I learned a lot more on my own. I am still learning.

I am not trying to portray these companies as bad or evil. But their primary interest is to sell their own products. It is not that you will be "taken," but they will not necessarily be doing what is best for you.

My advice is to use a discount brokerage firm such as Ameritrade, E-Trade, or Charles Schwab. They provide good advice without trying to push you into any one product. They also sell a wide variety of investment products. Make sure the broker or advisor with whom you are dealing sells a wide variety of products from many different companies. Pick up a copy of Money Magazine and check for listings of well-known mutual fund companies. If you have never dealt with a broker before, do not be intimidated. I can tell you from experience that I would much rather deal with someone that is new to investing and is interested in learning than someone with limited knowledge but believes he or she knows it all.

If a broker is constantly trying to move you from one product to another, something is wrong. This is called churning an account. The broker is simply trying to get more commissions out of you by buying and selling stocks or other investments. If this happens, get rid of that broker.

One last piece of advice – long-term financial planning means just that – it is long term. If you monitor your investments on a daily basis, you are going to drive yourself crazy. Not that you should not be aware, but one down day does not a trend make. In Peter Lynch's book, *One Up On Wall Street* he makes one of the best examples I have ever read. He points out that when we buy a house we check out the neighborhood, the schools, the stores and the condition of the house. We compare that house against others in the area. Once we buy, if the price of the house drops, we do not panic and sell, we ride it out. On the other hand, most people invest in stocks because "Joe at work told me we could make lots of money." Then, without doing any research, we just run out and buy. When the price drops, we sell and we lose.

I believe that 70% of investing is patience. The other 30% is good research with a little good luck thrown in. Most people lose on their investments because they buy high and sell low. That is not their plan, but they want a quick return and in doing so, they lose. I know one person who moves their 401(k) money to the mutual fund with the highest return during the prior quarter. Investments rarely have a steady, continuous return. They move up in a jagged line. The investment that does well this quarter, may do poorly over the next two quarters. When evaluating mutual funds, look at the prior 5-year return, not just how the fund performed over the last 3 to 12 months. Invest your money and be patient.

Excuse #3: "This is just way too complicated for me." No it is not. Just take it one step at a time. Ask questions, then ask even more questions. If you are not getting clear answers, ask someone else. If you feel like you are being pressured, back away. But do not quit. People, especially men it seems, are reluctant to let anyone know what they do not know about money and investing. Get over it. Get the information you need and get going.

OK, what do I do now?

- Know what you are investing in before you invest.
- For long-term investing, find a stock mutual fund that mirrors the S&P 500 stock index.
- Select the proper investment mix for you, depending on your age or length of the investment.
- Avoid inappropriate or "get rich quick" investments such as limited partnerships or options and futures.
- In general, use a large, discount brokerage firm such as E-Trade, Ameritrade, or Charles Schwab.

Chapter V

Life Insurance and Annuities

I am going to be honest. I do not especially like life insurance salespeople. I did not care for them before I got into financial planning and I liked them a lot less afterwards. The more I know, the less I like them.

There is definitely a need at some point in most people's lives for life insurance. But it seems that life insurance companies and salespeople find that all life's financial woes can be solved with, you guessed it, life insurance.

Despite what you may have been told or may be told in the future, there is no need to carry life insurance for your entire life. Cradle to old age coverage is simply not necessary, especially if you do even the most basic financial planning. Before buying any life insurance policy, ask yourself who would be adversely affected financially if you should die. Who is currently dependent upon your income or the services you provide (e.g. a stay-at-home parent) that if you died they would suffer financially. If the answer is "no one," then you probably do not need life insurance. Also, even if you need insurance now, that does not mean and should not mean that you need coverage for the rest of your life.

The one exception may be to own a small policy to cover funeral expenses for yourself and for your husband or wife. If you start an investment program and contribute diligently to that fund, even this would soon become unnecessary.

If you are married and especially if you have children at home or in college you probably should have life insurance. If you are the primary bread winner in the family, your death could be devastating. You need enough insurance coverage to keep your family going for quite some time after your death. Even couples that do not have children probably want to have both members insured especially if they have just bought a house and both incomes are needed to make the payments.

But, once the children are grown, the house is paid down, your house payment is no longer the major portion of your monthly expense, or you have retired, the need for life insurance decreases or simply goes away.

With that in mind, let's look at the different types of life insurance policies. Life insurance products can be basically placed in three categories: term life insurance, whole life or universal life products and annuities. Annuities are not actually life insurance but are sold under the same umbrella.

Term, Universal and Variable Universal Life Policies

Term life insurance covers only what is called the cost of insurance and associated fees. It is the same basic concept as buying car insurance. The premium amount you pay covers the cost of insurance and commissions to the salesperson with nothing left over. As you get older there is a greater chance that you will die, so, the premiums on term policies increase. If you cancel your policy, the premiums stop and you are no longer covered by the policy. Term life policies can be year to year or purchased for a guaranteed term of 5 to 30 years. A guaranteed term means that the premium amount remains the same for the specified length of the policy and the insurance company cannot cancel the policy even if your health should decline. But at the end of the term, if you decide to keep the policy in effect, the premiums will increase or you may not be able to continue the insurance at all should you not be in good health.

The next category of life insurance includes such names as whole life, universal life and variable universal life. The premiums on these policies are much higher than those of term life policies. These policies work under the assumption that you will keep the policy until you die, whether that be at age 30 or at age 90. So, the cost of insurance over the rest of your life is taken into consideration when calculating the premium amount. The premium amount is fixed for the life of the policy. The premium you pay covers the cost of insurance, management fees, and commissions to the salesperson with the remainder going into an investment account. In a whole life policy, the investment portion goes into the insurance company's general account. You are paid interest on the account and rates vary from year to year. In universal and variable universal life policies you are usually given investment options such as stock mutual funds. The investment portion acts as a reserve. As you get much older, your premium amount will no longer cover the cost of insurance. The additional amount required will be covered from the investment account.

Life insurance salespeople love to sell whole life and variable universal life policies. They do not like selling term life. One reason is that the commissions on whole life and universal life policies are much greater than the commissions on term policies. Their pitch is that you are getting life insurance and an investment. Plus, they will tell you, the investment is tax-deferred. So, if you live to age 65, the investment portion can be used to supplement your retirement income. Even better, they will say, if you "over-contribute" or pay more than the premium amount, the investment portion will grow even faster and you will have all this additional money later in life. If you cancel the policy you will be reimbursed the "cash surrender value" portion of the policy. Yes, this is all true, but you can do much better by buying a term policy and setting up your own investment program. Also, you need to fully understand what they mean by cash surrender value.

First of all, let's use a 38-year-old non-smoking male in our example. Currently, the premium for a 20-year guaranteed term policy with a face value of $100,000 is $20 a month. The premium for a variable universal life (VUL) policy is $80 a month. You would assume then that in the VUL policy that $60 a month would go towards the investment. Nope, it is less than that. Looking at a policy of a friend, only $46 a month goes toward the investment. The fees listed on the quarterly statement are Premium Expense Charges, Cost of Insurance Charges, and Monthly Expense Charges. What are all those fees? I honestly don't know. They add up to almost $34 a month. That alone is 70% higher than the premium on the term life policy.

The investment portion of the account is reflected on the statement as the "Accumulation Value" of the account. Remember our friendly life insurance salesperson said that if you cancel the policy, you get back the cash surrender value. Well, that is not the same thing as the accumulation value. In fact, depending on how many years you have held the policy, the cash surrender value may be zero. My friend is about six years into his policy and the cash surrender value is only 18% of the accumulation value. So, if his policy was "worth" $10,000 and he cancelled the policy, he would only be reimbursed $1,800!

If I read his policy correctly, the cash surrender value should equal the accumulation value in the twelfth year of the policy. Canceling the policy before that time just means more money in the pockets of the insurance company.

Using the above example, let's do a ten-year comparison between the term policy, matched with an investment you set up yourself and a whole life policy. In both cases, the monthly cost will be $80.

Policy Type	Face Amt	Prem. Per Mo.	Costs, Fees, etc.	Amt Toward Invest-ment	Value of Invest-ment
Term	$100,000	$80	$20	$60	$8,835
VUL	$100,000	$80	$34	$46	$6,773

At the end of the ten-year period, you will have paid $9,600 for each plan. Assuming that both your investment and the VUL averaged a 4% annual return, the VUL will have an accumulation value of $6,773 and your personal investment will have a value of $8,835. But, you may not actually get the entire $6,773 out of the VUL if you cancel the policy. Remember, surrender charges may apply. Even if there are no additional charges on the VUL, you will still have an additional $2,062 from your own investment.

Let's say that five years into the policy you decide you no longer need the insurance. Your rich Uncle Jim dies and leaves you $250,000. If you cancel the VUL or whole life policy, the accumulation value would be around $3,380. But, the cash surrender value would probably only be a fraction of that amount. On the other hand, if you cancel the term policy, your own investment account would be worth $4,400 and that is all yours to do with as you wish.

As far as using a life insurance policy as supplemental retirement savings, this makes no sense to me at all. First of all, if you contribute that same amount to your 401(k) plan, the contribution is tax deductible. This is not the case with the life insurance policy. Yes, the investment portion of the policy is a tax shelter, in that the growth is tax-deferred, but then so is your 401(k) or IRA. Plus, to get the full value of the life insurance account, the policy must stay in effect. This means that fees and possibly insurance costs will continue to come out of your investment and into the hands of the insurance company. Those fees are typically much greater than the management fees in a standard mutual fund.

I have also heard the sales pitch that you can borrow against your policy for retirement so that when you die, the policy covers the loan. Although there may be some good reasons to borrow from yourself, this is not one of them. As the accumulation value of the account decreases from the loan on the account, the costs of insurance are increasing because of your age. If you are 70 years old and are borrowing from your policy, the expenses to keep the policy alive are eating away at your investment.

Keep your life insurance needs and your investment needs separate. Do not let anyone sell you an investment wrapped in a life insurance policy. Any possible benefits, such as tax-deferred growth, are negated by the costs of insurance and any management fees. For example, do not buy life insurance on your children with the belief you are building an education fund. You do not need life insurance on your kids. If you want to start a college fund, open a bank savings account or a mutual fund and make regular deposits to the account. In a stock or equity mutual fund, a portion of the growth is also tax-deferred and the commissions are considerably less.

When looking at a term policy, first decide how long you are likely to need coverage. If you are planning to start a family, you probably want to look at guaranteed coverage for 25 to 30 years. Also, do not buy life insurance through your employer as your primary coverage unless you can keep that same coverage when you leave the company. Imagine taking out a $500,000 term life policy through your employer, getting so sick that you have to quit your job and because you left your job, your policy is cancelled. Just when you need life insurance the most, your coverage is terminated.

One more thing, *never* let anyone talk you into rolling your IRA or 401(k) account into a life insurance policy or annuity. In doing so, you are putting a tax shelter into another tax shelter. You are paying unnecessary fees and your investment options are limited. Also, you may be subject to surrender charges if you decide to move to another type of investment. These charges almost never apply to a bank or investment company IRA.

If you currently have a whole life, universal life, or variable universal life policy and you realize that it is not the best option for you, do not immediately run out and cancel the policy. First look at your term life insurance options. Term quotes are easily available from the internet. Go to any search engine (e.g. www.google.com) and type in "term life insurance quotes." There will be several sites from which to choose. They will ask you to enter your age, health, amount of insurance coverage, etc. and then will present you with quotes from several different companies. Be sure you can get the term coverage before canceling any other policies. Also, you need to look at the accumulation value in your current policy. If the accumulation value is substantially more than the cash surrender value, it may be in your best interest to simply hold on to the policy and re-evaluate your situation when the surrender value is close or equal to the accumulation value.

Annuities

Like IRA and 401(k) accounts, annuities are used for retirement planning. The growth of the account is tax-deferred and there are certain limits to withdrawing your money prior to retirement age. Unlike standard IRA and 401(k) accounts, the money you contribute to an annuity is not tax deductible but there is no limit to the amount you can place in the account during any one year. Also, the money you deposit into an annuity does not need to be earned income.

An annuity can be a useful tool if you have a large amount of money you want to protect until retirement age. For example, let's say when you turn 40 years old, Uncle Jim dies and leaves you $250,000. You decide you want to take $100,000 of that money and put it in a safe place for later in life. An annuity *may* be a good option. Like other life insurance products, the money deposited grows tax deferred and the account will usually provide you with several investment options. Annuities can also be useful for someone who has reached retirement age and wishes to shelter a certain amount of savings.

Upon reaching retirement, annuities offer several pay out options. The most common option is that the money is annuitized or amortized over the rest of your life. This means the insurance company, based on statistical charts, determines how long they expect you to live. They may base their calculations on the assumption that you will live another twenty years. They then take the value of your account, assume a certain interest rate, and then calculate how much they can pay you each month until you die. The advantage of this option is that if you beat the odds and live for another 40 years, the insurance company continues to pay you. The disadvantage is that if you die the following year, the balance of the account goes to the insurance company. There are other options, such as "ten year period certain," which means the account will pay out until your death or for the next ten years, which ever comes last. So, if you die one year after annuitizing the account, the insurance company will continue making the monthly payments to your designated beneficiary for the next nine years for a total of ten years. If you live longer than 10 years, the annuity will continue making payments until your death.

There is usually also an option that allows a lump sum pay out from the account. In many ways, this is the most important option. The reason it is so important is that I found it is a good way for me, as a financial planner, to gauge the flexibility of the annuity. One thing annuities are infamous for is their exorbitant penalties for withdrawing your money from the account, especially prior to retirement. Like whole and universal life policies, there is an accumulation value and a surrender value. In many policies, over several years, the surrender value will eventually equal the accumulation value. In many bad policies, that never happens. If you decide to take your money out in a lump sum or roll the money into another annuity, the insurance company will keep a substantial portion of your account.

The best annuity I dealt with allowed the owner of the annuity to withdraw up to 20% of the account each year for the first five years without a penalty. After the five-year period, the accumulation and surrender values were equal and all money could be withdrawn. Let me re-emphasize that, by law, penalties may apply prior to retirement age, regardless of the annuity. I am specifically speaking of the penalties imposed by the insurance company. Some annuities did not allow total access to your money until the twelfth or even the fifteenth year.

When reviewing annuities owned by clients or friends, the first thing I look at is how available is their money should they need to withdraw it from the account. What penalties may apply? In every case where a client's annuity never allowed complete withdrawal of the money, I would ask them, "Did your insurance agent cover the penalties on this account if you decide to withdraw the money? Did he tell you that the entire balance of the account would never be available to you unless you annuitize the account? Did he compare this annuity with annuities offered by other companies?" The answer to these questions were always "No." And that is why I do not like life insurance salespeople.

Annuities should never be used as your primary retirement savings. If you are still working, always use an IRA from a bank or brokerage company or a 401(k) account from your employer. The money you contribute to those accounts is most likely tax deductible, unlike an annuity. Annuities can be used for IRAs, but do not go there. There is no benefit to placing IRA money into an annuity. In fact, the commissions paid out to the insurance company and salespeople can be outrageous. You do not see that side of it though. The salesperson is not required to cover the commission structure with you. Sales commissions on most insurance products are hidden. Mutual funds are required to fully disclose all commissions and management fees. Do not let any salesperson of any type ever tell you that there are no commissions. No one works for free.

School Teachers and TSA (403(b)) Accounts

Since annuities may be the only option for teachers and non-profit organization employees, be careful about which company you deal with. Your first question should be, "What penalties will apply should I later decide to roll this money into an IRA or into another annuity?" It is not unreasonable for there to be a period of three to seven years in which penalties will apply. Anything longer is not acceptable. Before signing an annuity contract, make the agent show you in the contract where withdrawal penalties are discussed. Be sure he shows you where it is written when, if at all, all of your money will be available to you.

So, are annuities bad? No, they can be useful tools. But, before putting any money into an annuity, be sure you understand all of the limitations of the policy. I can pretty much guarantee you that the agent will not offer this information without you asking. But even if you ask, he will probably not compare his product with products from other insurance companies. Investment brokers also sell annuities and offer them from several insurance companies. An agent representing only one company will give you only one option.

If you are currently contributing to an annuity, especially a TSA account and realize you could do better elsewhere, simply stop contributing to the current TSA. Find another agent or broker and check into other options. You may not be able to easily roll your money out of the original annuity, but at least you have started contributing to a better plan.

Excuse #4: "I bought my policies from a friend. I don't want to cancel them and hurt his feelings." I could not believe how often I heard this excuse. I am not accusing your friend of taking advantage of you. Most likely, he was simply doing what he was taught by the company for which he works. On the other hand, *your* life and *your* money are *your* responsibility. You have got to do what is best for *you*. If making changes to your insurance or investment portfolio makes sense, then make the change. I guarantee you that you will not be the first client your friend has lost.

OK, what do I do now?
- Buy life insurance only if someone is dependent upon your income (such as your family).
- Buy only term life insurance. Avoid whole life, universal life and variable universal life.
- Keep your life insurance needs and your investment needs separate.
- **DO NOT** use life insurance as an investment vehicle.
- **NEVER** use life insurance policies for your retirement accounts (e.g. IRA).
- Have full knowledge of annuity surrender charges before investing.

Chapter VI

Buying A Car

Buying a car is one of the most intimidating experiences any of us will ever have to go through. We know we are getting taken to the cleaners and yet most of us do not know what to do about it. I was lucky. I did not have to actually go in and buy a car until I was 38 years old. My father (the CPA) had clients that owned car dealerships. I would call a client of Dad's, tell them what I wanted and then pick it up. After Dad retired, I was on my own. But, as I mentioned in the Introduction, a good friend of mine worked as a car salesman and in the finance office. I talked to him a long time before I ever walked into a dealership and began negotiations.

Negotiating does not come naturally to me. If you are like me, or even if you do know a thing or two about negotiating, I strongly recommend you first read the classic book *You Can Negotiate Anything* by Herb Cohen. Not only will it help you with purchases, it can also help you in your career.

I am not willing to haggle at a swap meet over 50 cents. I would rather just pay and be done. But I know that not being prepared before entering a car dealership could cost me an additional $4,000 to $5,000. I have to work a lot of hours for that much money. This means that being prepared before visiting a dealer, even if it takes an additional 2 to 3 hours, could mean saving the equivalent of over $1,000 an hour for my time. I don't know about you, but that is good money to me.

I live in Southern California. Our lives revolve around our cars. We often dream about what it must be like to own a different car. Since our emotions get wrapped up in our cars, our brains tend to shut off when we go to buy one, which leads us to do all of the wrong things. Car salespeople know this. They know when we walk into a dealership we basically have a sign on our forehead that says, "Take advantage of me!"

Buying a car does not need to be a nerve racking or intimidating experience. Like almost anything in life, you just need to be prepared. You need to know the salesperson's game plan. Once you know it, you can be in control of the situation and have the confidence you need to get a good deal.

Step 1 – Identify the Make and Model of the Car You Want to Buy

If you are not sure of the specific make and model of car you want, please go car shopping. But do not under any circumstances buy a car on that outing. You will be pressured, but do not give in. You have work ahead of you before you are ready to sign a sales contract. Never believe the pitch "this price is good for today only." Car dealers always want to sell cars. Tomorrow is just as good a day as today.

Step 2 – Get Information on the Dealer's Invoice Price

Once you have determined which model you want, you need to find out the dealer's invoice price for that model. The invoice price is the amount the dealer paid for the car. Do not confuse this price with the sticker price or the manufacturer's suggested retail price (MSRP). The easiest way to get the invoice price is to log on to the internet, go to a search engine (e.g. www.google.com) and type in "new car invoice prices" as your search criteria. This will bring up several websites that you can use to find the invoice price of the car. You can also check Kelly Blue Book (www.kbb.com) and Consumer Reports websites. The invoice price from these sites is not necessarily the actual price the dealer paid for the car. The dealer may also get rebates from the manufacturer. But, the invoice price from any one of these websites gives you a good idea of the amount the dealer paid.

Many of these same websites also give quotes on retail prices and will put you in touch with a specific dealer. Some dealers even have their own websites where you can select your car and get a price quote immediately. This is extremely beneficial as you will have a quote you can use to compare against when talking to other dealers.

Step 3 – Check the Reliability of the Model You Want to Purchase

When checking out different makes and models of cars, be sure to look at their repair history and their residual or trade-in values. Consumer Reports magazine and website regularly rates the dependability of various models of cars. If the car in which you are interested is likely to require a lot of repairs, you may want to consider something else. Also, the trade-in value of a car is very important. A friend and I bought cars about a year apart. Recently, we checked the Kelly Blue Book for the wholesale and retail values of our cars. My car was older, had many more miles on it (almost 80,000 more), and I paid less for it than he paid for his. Six years later, mine was worth $4,000 more than his. This may not seem important when you are buying a car, but it will seem extremely important when you go to sell it or trade it in for your next car.

Step 4 – Look Into Financing

The next thing you need to do is to check into financing. Check with your bank and/or credit union. Credit unions often offer some of the best rates on car loans. Find out what interest rate they will charge you, the term of the loan and how much money they will lend. Get pre-approval on the loan, if possible. Dealerships may offer low interest rates in their ads, but they can be misleading. They may require you to have a high credit score on your credit report or the loan may only be for 12 to 24 months. Never assume the dealer is going to offer you a good deal on financing.

Step 5 – Investigate the Value of Your Used Car

The final step before enter a dealership is to look into the current value of your used car if you intend to sell or trade it in. Again, check on the internet. Kelly Blue Book is probably the best-known source of used car pricing and information. Their web site is www.kbb.com. The price you get from this site is the retail price. Realize that a dealer will only give you a fraction of that amount.

Ideally, you should sell your used car yourself. Car dealers are going to give you as little as possible for your trade-in. But, I also realize that most people do not want the inconvenience of selling their car. Just realize that the cost of the convenience of trading the car in at the dealership is high.

Now you are ready to enter the dealership. Remember, you are the customer. They need you to buy a car to stay in business. You, on the other hand, can always go to another dealer. You do not "owe" them anything.

Step 6 – Let the Negotiations Begin!

Once you start looking seriously at a car the salesperson will ask you, "How much do you want your monthly payment to be?" OK, stop right there! What did I tell you in Chapter II of this book? **Never, never buy anything based solely on the monthly payment amount.** Even if you know what is the maximum amount you can afford for a monthly payment, do not tell the salesperson.

There are three points to negotiate in the purchase of a car. Only negotiate one item at a time and only negotiate in the following order.

1. **Price of the car**
2. **Interest rate and term of financing**
3. **Amount they will pay you for your trade in.**

If you cannot reach an agreement on the price of the car, do not let the salesperson start talking to you about your trade in or about financing. If necessary, go to another dealer.

Tell the salesperson you have already secured financing on the new car and you will not be trading in your old car. The only thing you are interested in negotiating is price. Car salespeople want to wear you down. They want you to invest a lot of time in the negotiating process. Why? Because they are hoping you will think, "I have invested a lot of time in this, I am not leaving here without a new car." That attitude is bad for you and good for them. Just turn that around and remember that the salesperson also has just invested a lot of time in the transaction. He or she does not want you to leave either. So, stay firm on your price. Do not tolerate a salesperson whining at you. One of my least favorite lines is "I am not making any money on this as it is! I can't go any lower!" Yeah, right. Remember, their commission is not your problem.

After agreeing on the price of the car, say to the salesperson, "You know, I have already secured financing through my bank, but what interest rate and term can you give me?" At first, do not tell the salesperson the rate you were quoted from your bank. Let them offer their rate. If your bank's rate is lower, then offer the information and see if they can come back with even better terms. Often auto manufacturers will offer special rates on certain models. If the rate is better than the one you are getting from the bank, take it. Just be sure that what is written on the sales and financing contract is exactly what you agreed to during negotiations. Numbers have been known to change when the documents are drawn up.

Now, after agreeing on the interest rate and term, say to the salesperson, "You know, maybe I don't want to hold on to the old car. How much will you give me for it?" By now, steam should be coming out of the salesperson's ears. If he or she is mad, you are probably doing a very good job.

Their strategy is to just keep talking about the monthly payment amount, just like the example I gave in Chapter II of the big screen television. But, with a car, it can get even more interesting. They can manipulate the price of the car, the interest rate, the length of the loan, and the amount they are giving you for your trade-in.

Let's say you are looking at a car with a sticker price of $22,000. You have an older model car you think might be worth $2,000. You want to use the money you receive for the old car as your down payment on the new car. The dealer initially quotes you a payment amount of $475 a month. That is more than you want to pay, you tell him. He goes back and discusses it with the manager and comes back with a new amount of $431 a month. You hold your ground and force him to go back and bring it down even lower. He finally comes back, gives you a sad story that they are not making money on this deal and quotes you $409 a month. That sounds pretty good to you, so you take the deal. How did you make out? Well, the guys at the dealership are still laughing and telling stories about you.

Car Price	Trade-in Amt	Amt Financed	Int Rate	Term (yrs)	Pmt Amt	Total of all Pmts
$22,000	$2,000	$20,000	6.5%	4	$474	$22,766
$23,000	$1,500	$21,500	7.5%	5	$430	$25,849
$24,000	$1,000	$23,000	8.5%	6	$408	$29,440

Each time the payment amount went down they were actually *increasing* the price of the car, *decreasing* the amount they were giving you for your trade-in, *increasing* the interest rate and *increasing* the term of the loan. You are just the kind of person that salespeople love to "negotiate" with.

Although this is an extreme example, I hope it makes you at least a little angry. In fact, I hope it makes you angry enough that you never again let yourself get taken by a salesperson. I hope you never negotiate anything based on the monthly payment amount alone.

However, the reality is that people do think in terms of monthly payments because that is how their money is budgeted. So, if I know I can afford a monthly car payment of $350, then how do I know how much I can afford to spend on a car? The best thing to do is to get a calculator that amortizes loans. If you do not want to do that, check on the internet. Go to a search engine such as www.yahoo.com and type in "amortization calculator." There are basically four pieces to the puzzle: the interest rate, the length or term of the loan, the amount you are borrowing and the payment amount. If you have any three of these items, the calculator can give you the fourth. In the above example, let's say you know you want a four year or 48 month loan and your bank is offering you an interest rate of 6%. Enter your $350 a month payment, the 4-year term and the 6% loan rate and you will find you can afford a $14,900 car. Try several different scenarios so you will be prepared when you enter the car dealership.

The Finance Office

My friend, the ex-car salesman also told me horror stories from the finance office. Once you finally settle on the terms of the deal, they take you to meet the finance manager so that he can write it up. While you are in his office, the manager is going to try to sell you all kinds of additional warranties, treatments, insurance, and so on. My friend basically said, "Do not buy anything from the finance manager, no matter how good it sounds. You are getting taken." Now, I am not sure this is true about everything they might try to sell you, but it is a good rule of thumb. They will tell you that extended warranties sell for $600, but they will be good enough to sell it to you for $300. The dealer probably paid only $75 for the same warranty.

When I bought my last car the finance manager tried to sell me some sort of insurance that should my car be stolen, would pay for a rental car. To deter theft, they would also etch the vehicle identification number (VIN) on each window in the car. I said no. When I got the car, I discovered the manufacturer had already etched the VIN on each window. They were trying to sell me something that was already on the car!

In my opinion, you should never finance a car for longer than four years. If you accept a loan longer than four years, it is too likely you will end up upside-down in the loan. This means that you may owe more on the car than the car is worth. If you need to sell the car before the end of the loan, the amount you get from the sale of the car will not be enough to pay off the loan. If you cannot afford the payment of a four-year loan and need a longer loan period, you probably cannot actually afford the car.

Used Cars

Buying a used car is much like buying a new one except you will not be able to get good information on how much the dealer actually paid for the car. You can get an idea of the retail value of the car from Kelly Blue Book, but that is not going to give you the full story. There are also internet companies (e.g. www.carfax.com) that can provide you with background information on a specific car. This can be helpful in determining whether or not a car has been in a major accident. To retrieve this information, you will need the VIN or vehicle identification number from the specific car you are considering to purchase. The VIN is a seventeen character identifier that can be found on dashboards, the driver's side door jamb stickers and on title documents.

Many car companies now offer used cars with warranties similar to those offered on new cars. They will take automobiles that have previously been on lease programs, give them a good once over and then sell them under "certified" or "preferred" used cars or "previously-owned" programs. The biggest advantage of buying a used car is that you are letting the original owner take the biggest hit on the depreciation of the car. Luxury leased cars usually have low miles and have been well maintained. In my opinion, you should always check into this type of option before buying a new car.

Leasing a Car

Should you buy or should you lease? If you feel you need a new car every year and have lots of money to throw around, leasing might work for you. But if you live in the real world like me, leasing does not make a lot of sense. Unfortunately, most people lease cars because they cannot afford to buy the car they actually want. At the end of the lease, they have nothing to show for their months of high payments.

I cannot see any advantages to leasing a car for *personal* use. Buy a car, take care of it, pay it off and hold on to it. If you cannot afford to buy it, you cannot afford it at all.

If you own a business there may be some advantages to leasing a car rather than owning it. But before signing any lease, discuss the tax advantages or disadvantages with your accountant.

But, with that said, some of you will still be lured into leasing a car. If this is the path you intend to take, let's go over some of the elements of auto leasing.

Since you do not actually own a leased car, your lease payments are paying for the depreciation of the car as well as profit to the owner of the vehicle. The company leasing you the car first calculates the residual value of the car. The residual value is what they estimate the car will be worth at the end of the lease. The difference between the current value of the car and the residual value, plus profit is the basis of your lease payment. One element used to calculate the residual value is the number of miles they estimate you will put on the car. This amount is usually limited to 12,000 to 15,000 a year. If you drive more miles than the amount specified in the lease, you will be charged for each mile over the maximum at the end of the lease. Usually this amount runs ten to fifteen cents a mile. This may not sound like much, but if like me you are more apt to drive 24,000 miles a year and you have a two-year lease you may end up owing an additional $3,600 when you return the car.

Surprisingly, even though you are not purchasing the car, you still have to pay sales tax when leasing a car. You will also be required to pay the state license fees as well as maintenance and insurance, all as if you actually owned it.

When selecting a lease, be sure to avoid terms such as 13, 25 or 37 months. This is a way the leasing company gets you to pay one more year of the license fees, just before you turn in the car. Make sure the term is in one year or twelve month increments. Another caveat is to avoid open-end leases, always be sure that the lease is closed-end. An open-end lease allows the leasing company to set the residual value of the car at the end of the lease, rather than at the beginning. In many cases, the car may be worth much less than the residual value calculated at the beginning of the lease. If the lease is open-ended, you will be responsible for paying for that difference. This could end up being a big, unpleasant surprise when you turn in the car.

When the term of your lease is up, also compare the residual value stated in your lease agreement against the actual value of the car. In certain cases, the leased car may be in high demand and the car is worth much more than the residual value in the contract. If the difference is great enough, it may be best to buy the car out of the lease and sell it yourself.

Be aware, if you decide to buy the car out of the lease, you will once again be charged sales tax. Depending upon the value of the car and the sales tax rate in your state this could add an additional $1,000 to $3,000 to the cost.

If you insist on leasing a car because you "just have to have it," I feel it is better to purchase the car and take a six-year term on the car loan. This breaks my rule from above, but at least you will own the car and potentially avoid additional sales tax and license fees.

Excuse #5: "I don't have the time to spend doing all that research." I recently went with a friend when he bought a new car. By the time we were done negotiating, the price of the car had dropped over $4,000. The first $2,000 fell off the price quickly. The second $2,000 took another hour. He probably spent a total of three hours between research and the actual negotiations. If you do not think that spending three hours of your time is worth it to save $4,000, then you probably do not need to be reading this book.

OK, what do I do now?
- Investigate the car you want to buy including the dealer's invoice price
- Get a quote on your own financing
- Investigate the value of your used car
- Negotiate sales price, interest rate of financing, and trade-in value separately and in that order
- **NEVER negotiate monthly payment amount**
- Avoid purchases from the finance office
- Avoid leasing a car for personal use

Chapter VII

Buying a House

Next to retirement planning, buying a house is probably the most important investment and financial decision you will ever make. It is a big decision and a big responsibility – but it is worth it.

Research and planning are extremely important before buying a house. Even if you are not yet ready to buy, you need to start planning for the future purchase of one now. The more you know, the better your preparation, the easier it will be for you to get into your new home.

Reasons to buy a house

There are three main advantages to buying a house:
- **Fixed Monthly Payments**
- **Building Equity**
- **Tax Relief**

If you are renting a house or apartment, your monthly payment can change from month to month or year to year depending on the terms of your lease. Plus, the amount you pay is not deductible on your tax return. When you leave the rental unit, all of your rent payments have gone to the owner of the building – you get nothing back.

By buying, you build equity or value in your home in two ways. The first is by slowly paying off the principal of the loan. The second is from appreciation of the value of the property. Over the long term, property values have consistently risen. There will be times when property values fall, but since a house should always be viewed as a long term investment, short term fluctuations in the market are just that – they are short term.

Although there are many types of loans available when purchasing a home, the most common is a 30-year fixed loan. This means the interest rate is fixed for the life of the loan, which is, not surprisingly, 30 years. Instead of facing periodic increases in the rent on your apartment, the monthly loan payment on your house for this type of loan will remain constant for 30 years. I will go into more details about the different types of loans available later in this chapter.

The interest portion of the loan payment is deductible on your federal income taxes and usually your state income taxes. This provides a tremendous savings that helps make up the initial difference in the monthly payment between your apartment rent and your house payment. Monthly tax savings is completely dependent upon your income and how much interest you pay on the loan each month. But, assuming a $200,000, 30-year loan at 6% interest rate, you should be able to save somewhere between $200 and $400 a month in taxes. You do not need to wait until the end of each year to get these benefits, either. By adjusting the number of dependents you claim on your Form W-4 through your employer's payroll department, you can immediately decrease the amount of taxes withheld from your paycheck. This money will then be available to make your monthly house payment.

Although you should consult with your accountant or other tax professional, adjusting your W-4 deductions is completely legal as long as your intent is not to defraud the government. The worksheet provided with your W-4 is to be used as a guide only. If you have been receiving very large tax refund amounts you should immediately increase the number of your W-4 deductions. As long as you don't owe the government a large amount of money at the end of the year for taxes, this is perfectly legal. You may also change the number of deductions more than once a year, if you see the need.

It is important not to wait to buy a house or condominium. The longer you wait, the more difficult it will be. As out of reach buying a house may seem, the "reach" will keep getting longer the longer you wait. Let me give you an example of what I mean by this.

Bill and Janet decide they would like to buy a house. They want the payment to be as low as possible. They find a house they like for $200,000. Bill and Janet start saving money to put toward the down payment. They want to save at least $20,000 or 10% of the purchase price of their new home. The problem is that while they are trying to save the

$20,000 their target keeps moving away from them. Bill and Janet are aggressive savers and are able to put away $1,000 a month toward their new home. But by the time they save up the $20,000, the house they want is now selling for $240,000. In the mean time, their rent increased $70 a month and for the 20 months it took them to save the money, they did not get any sort of tax deduction on their rent.

If you are looking at your first home purchase, what is most important is to just take the plunge and buy. The difference between putting 5% and 10% down on a house will not significantly change the monthly payment. In Bill and Janet's case, assuming a 6% interest rate, putting 10% down on a $200,000 house would give them a monthly payment of $1,140. If they put only 5% down, their payment would be $1,180, a difference of only $40 a month. In some cases, especially for first time home buyers, it is possible to buy a house without putting any money down. You may pay a slightly higher interest rate, but it may be worth it. Some cities also have first time home buyer programs which may offer lower interest rates or may finance part of the down payment.

Throughout this chapter I will often refer to the monthly payment amount. I know that in the previous chapters I have said never buy anything based on the monthly payment. I am not making an exception to that rule in this chapter. Houses are not sold based on a monthly payment. You negotiate the price of the house with the seller and the loan is handled by a broker or bank who sets the interest rate. After agreeing on a price and finding a rate on a loan you will then know the amount of the monthly payment and whether or not it will work within your budget.

The process of buying a house varies from state to state. Some states require you to hire an attorney to represent your interests in the sale or purchase of a house. Although the topics discussed below are common to most real estate transactions, be sure to research what is required in your state before jumping into a home purchase.

Even though the following information should give you a good overview, I strongly recommend you do more research before buying a house. The website of the U.S. Government Housing and Urban Development (www.hud.gov) provides helpful information for free. Also check out the Fannie Mae web page for information on home loans (www.fanniemae.com). There are many books available on this subject. If you live in California, you might read *How To Buy A House in*

California by Ralph E. Warner, George Devine, and Ira Serkes. Your city, county and state government offices may also offer valuable information.

Real Estate Agents

A real estate agent is usually the first person you contact when you begin looking to buy a house. As a buyer, it costs you nothing to be represented by an agent. The agent makes his or her money from the seller of the house, providing the seller lists their property with their own real estate agent. Try to find an agent with whom you feel comfortable. A good agent should try to learn what types of homes interest you. He or she should preview different homes prior to showing them to you. If an agent tries to push you into buying a house you do not like or continues to show you homes that do not meet your criteria, get another agent. This is a big decision and a big investment. You do not want someone pushing you into a home that is not a good fit. Your agent should respect your wishes and your time. On the other hand, try also to respect your agent's time. Do not ask to be shown homes that you cannot afford or that you are simply curious about.

Many people often shop for new homes during an "open house." This is when the seller and the seller's agent have the house open for anyone to have a look around. The seller's agent is usually present to answer questions. If you are interested in the property, the agent will be only too happy to represent you as well. In general, I recommend against this. Find an agent to represent your interests as the buyer and let the other agent represent the seller's interests.

Once you decide on a home, your agent will help you make an offer on the property. It is common that after an offer is made, the owner will make a counter offer. The counter offer will be presented to you by your agent and then, if you wish, you can counter the counter offer. For example, you find a house you like with an asking price of $200,000. You offer the seller $190,000 for the house. The owner then counters your offer with $195,000. You can counter that offer, accept it, or walk away. There are many more elements of the sale besides just the selling price of the house that may enter into negotiations.

Do not rely on your agent to hold your hand and help you through the entire process of buying a house. Many will provide some assistance and advice, but an agent's job is primarily to sell houses. Once you have made an offer on a property and the offer is accepted, in many ways, your agent's job is complete. Your agent may be knowledgeable and helpful during the loan process but he or she is not the actual loan agent. Your agent is not an employee of the escrow company or the title company. It is your responsibility to ensure that the deal on your home moves forward.

As the real estate market has changed, so have real estate agents and brokers. Many sellers now list their homes with brokers that charge lower fees than traditional companies. The lower fees paid by the sellers can mean lower commissions to the buying agent. This means that your agent may be motivated to only show you homes in which he or she gets the highest commission rate. Because of this, you need to be proactive and look for homes yourself. Not surprisingly, the internet has become an excellent market for homes. With photos and virtual tours available on many sites, you can often preview homes before actually visiting them. You can also search based on your specific criteria. Visit sites such as www.realtor.com, www.fsbo.com and search on www.google.com for other real estate sites. If you find houses that you like, tell your real estate agent that you would like to see these homes as well. If the agent hesitates to show you the homes, find another agent.

I will talk more about low fee real estate brokers in the section below on Selling a House.

Lenders

The second entity you are likely to work with in purchasing a house is a lender. The most common types of lenders are banks, credit unions and mortgage brokers (mortgage bankers). A mortgage broker is independent and represents one or more lending institutions. He or she is paid a commission on your loan from the lender. One advantage of using brokers is that they do a lot of the leg work for you. Brokers try to find the lowest rates among many different lenders. If you have less than perfect credit or need your financing to be somewhat "creative," they may know of lenders that work with those types of borrowers. If you work directly with a bank or credit union, you will need to shop for the best rate and terms yourself.

Both have their advantages and disadvantages. Banks and credit unions tend to be more straightforward. They present their rates, terms and conditions and go from there. You tend to need to keep a closer watch on a broker. Rates and terms can quickly change, often at the last minute.

The loan process is one place where your home purchase can go seriously awry. Delays in getting loan approval can cause serious problems. There are often clauses in the purchase agreement where the seller of the house can back out of the deal if your loan is not funded in a timely manner. It is extremely important that you have everything in order before applying for a loan. Make sure that your credit report is clean. If there are any problems with the report, try to get them cleared up, if possible. Make sure you have copies of your most recent pay stubs available. You will also need copies of tax returns for the prior two years. Make a list of your past employers and places you have lived over the last 10 years. Most importantly, you will need available cash, the more the better.

Most home purchases try to close within 30 days of the acceptance of the offer by the seller. This may seem like a long time if you have never before bought a house, but it is not. So much has to happen within those 30 days that there is little time for problems to be resolved. You cannot be too prepared when beginning this process.

Although 30-day escrow periods are the most common, the length of the escrow can be longer or even shorter depending on the situation of the seller and the buyer. Escrows can be 30, 45, 60 or even 90 days in length. Longer escrows are often requested by the seller while he or she continues to look for a new home to purchase.

Everyone, from you to the seller to the real estate agent to the bank or loan broker has a serious financial interest in completing this transaction. You will tend to have an emotional investment in the purchase. People find a house they like and they do not want to lose it. This works against you as the buyer, especially if the loan broker you are working with is not completely above board.

About five years ago I was renting an apartment while looking for a place to buy. After looking at many places I finally found a great condominium. It was by far the best I had seen. I went through a loan broker who was recommended to me by my real estate agent. My loan would require both a first and a second mortgage (I will go into this more in the Financing segment of this chapter). She quoted the rate on the first at 7 ¼% and on the second at 11%. About ten days before the loan was to close, she called me and said the lender had given her incorrect information and the actual rates would be 8 ¼% on the first and 10% on the second. But, she assured me, the total mortgage payment would be "only" an additional $100 a month. She knew I was close to moving into the new place. She knew I had given notice at my apartment. She knew she had me between a rock and a hard place. Much like the salesperson in the finance office of a car dealership she was trying to squeeze a higher rate out of me that would give her a higher commission. As much as I wanted that house, I knew I had to be prepared to walk away from the deal. In the purchase offer to the seller, I made sure there was a clause that if the mortgage rate was higher than 7 ½% I could walk away without penalties. So, I told the loan broker that if she did not immediately find me a better rate I would back out of the deal and find another house. She was counting on me to roll over and accept the new rate, as many people do. I didn't. Not surprisingly, she came up with a much better loan package.

A neighbor of mine owns an escrow company. He told me one way to keep loan brokers honest is to apply with both a broker and with a bank. Tell both lenders that you have also applied with the other and whoever gets the loan approved on time with the best rate gets your business. It may cost you more to do this, but it tends to keep the loan broker honest. If he knows you can drop him at any time and give the bank your business, he is less likely to try to pull a "bait and switch" at the last minute.

When your lender needs information from you, provide it, as soon as possible. You may be asked to provide pay stubs, and then two weeks later, provide them again. It is not unusual, especially for first time home buyers to be asked to provide lots of seemingly unnecessary information. Keep your cool and just give them what they require.

Keep a friendly and also close relationship with your lender. You are just one of many loans he or she is handling. If you do not hear from him or her for several days, give a call to "just touch base" and make sure there is not anything additional they need from you.

Escrow Companies

Escrow companies, by definition, are impartial third parties that act upon instructions for both the seller and the buyer as well as the borrower and the lender. They act as a middleman, ensuring that all required documents and procedures are properly brought together and completed. They also act as a type of bank. Monies flow through the escrow company between the buyer and seller. Not all states require escrow companies in the process of the sale. If yours does, it is also a good idea to find out who is assigned to your file at the escrow company and keep a "close and friendly" relationship with that person as well. In fact, when I sold and bought my last houses, I insisted that the same escrow company as well as the same representative handle both transactions. This gave me one point of contact on both deals. Everything came together perfectly and I bought the escrow representative a bottle of champagne to thank her for all of her help.

If you are selling and buying a house at the same time, another advantage of using the same escrow company for both transactions is that you can ask for a discount on the escrow fees. The savings on both sides of the deal can amount to several hundred dollars.

Three terms often used regarding escrow are "open escrow," "in escrow" and "close of escrow." Usually you have to deposit money into an escrow account to open escrow on the transaction. Between opening escrow and the completion of the deal, it is said that the house is "in escrow." When escrow closes, the house is yours.

Title Insurance

Title insurance protects the buyer and lender of a property against any unknown "defect of title." After you purchase the property, if somehow there is a problem with the title or ownership of the property, the title insurance company will provide you with compensation and/or representation against any possible lawsuits. Shortly after close of escrow, you will receive a title insurance policy. Keep this policy in a safe place with all other important documents from the transaction.

The policy premium is a one-time fee that is paid out of escrow funds, usually by the seller of the property.

Unlike the loan agent and the escrow representative, you probably will not have any direct contact with anyone at the title insurance company. Your escrow representative will usually be the one to handle this and ensure that all paperwork is properly received so escrow can close on time.

Financing

Home loans come in a variety of packages. Most are either fixed or variable and have terms from 10 to 30 years, usually in five-year increments (10, 15, 20, 25, and 30).

In a fixed loan the interest rate you pay remains the same or level for the life of the loan. The interest rate in a variable or adjustable rate mortgage (ARM) loan changes periodically based on current rates in the debt markets. There are advantages and disadvantages to both types of loans, although fixed rate loans are more common than variable interest rate loans.

There are also loans called balloon mortgages. These loans often have low interest rates fixed for the first 3 to 7 years. At the end of the term, the entire loan must be refinanced or paid off. This type of loan should only be considered if you know for certain that you will be selling the property before the end of the term of the loan. The only other time this type of loan *might* be attractive is if mortgage rates in general are trending lower and you expect to refinance the loan before the end of the term of the balloon mortgage.

Variable rate loans usually have lower interest rates than fixed loans. The disadvantage is that as interest rates rise, so will your mortgage payment. This could potentially cause your monthly payment to increase by several hundred dollars over the years. The advantage is that if you buy a house during a time when interest rates are high, your payment will decrease as interest rates begin to fall. If you are buying a house when interest rates are low, it is almost always best to choose a fixed rate loan.

There are also loans available in which you pay only the interest portion of the loan. Since you are only paying interest and no principal, your monthly payment will be lower than a more conventional type loan. These loans should be avoided. In using this type of loan, you are viewing your house as a speculative investment rather than a conservative home purchase. These loans are usually variable rate loans and often must be paid off after 3 to 7 years. If interest rates have risen (which they are likely to do after being so low for so long) and this same type of loan is no longer available, the payments on a fixed rate loan or more traditional variable rate loan could be more than you could afford. If you cannot afford a home with a fixed or traditional type ARM, do not buy the house.

The longer the term of the loan, the lower the monthly payment. The shorter the term, the higher the monthly payment but you will also pay less over the life of the loan. Let's assume you purchase a house and need to finance $175,000 and the current interest rate is 6%. Here are the changes in payment amounts based on the term of the loan.

Term of Loan	Monthly Payment	Total Payments
30	$1,049.21	$377,716.83
25	$1,127.53	$338,258.24
20	$1,253.75	$300,901.04
15	$1,476.75	$265,814.90

You can see if you choose a term of 15 years over 30 your monthly payments will be $428 higher. But, over the life of the loan you will pay $111,902 less using the 15-year mortgage. Realistically, for the average first time home buyer, you will probably need to find the lowest monthly payment possible. As you build equity in your house and should you later look into refinancing, it is wise to consider loans with shorter terms. Shorter term loans often carry lower interest rates as well.

A first mortgage is the primary mortgage on your house. It does not refer to the first time you borrow money to buy real estate. Your property can be used as collateral in more than one mortgage. The first mortgage has the highest or first claim against the property in the case of a default. The second mortgage is subordinate to the first and usually carries a higher interest rate than the first mortgage. It is important to be familiar with these terms. In home purchases with small down payments, it is sometimes advantageous to finance 80% of the purchase with a first mortgage and the remainder with a second.

If more than 80% of the cost of the house is financed (i.e., you put less than 20% down) the lender will usually require private mortgage insurance (PMI). This insurance protects the lender against loss should you default on the loan. The premiums are usually added to your monthly mortgage payment. Although you pay the premiums on this insurance, it protects the lender, not you. After you have owned the property for a while and have made all of your payments on time, you can request that the lender drop the PMI. If the property has increased in value such that the balance of the loan represents 80% or less of the value of the house, the lender will likely honor the request. If they do not, look into refinancing the house with another lender.

After purchasing and moving into your new home, prevailing mortgage interest rates may fall lower then your current rate. When this happens, it may be to your advantage to refinance your home. This means you find (usually) a new lender, take out a new loan and pay off the old loan. With a lower interest rate, your monthly payment is also lower. The concept of refinancing to a lower rate is usually a good idea. On the other hand, there are some things to consider before rushing out and refinancing.

1. Many loans require points, fees and/or closing costs. These costs can range from a few hundred dollars to several thousand. If you pay $2,400 in closing costs on the new loan and your payment drops $100 a month, it is going to take two years before you recover those costs. There are loans available for refinancing where all costs are either rolled into the loan, which increases your principal balance, or you pay a slightly higher interest rate than if you paid the costs upfront. The last option, in a way, makes refinancing free. It definitely makes the decision much easier, but you will never get the lowest mortgage rate with this type of loan.

2. If you have been paying on your 30-year mortgage for 7 years and refinance back into another 30-year mortgage, your monthly payment may be lower, but you have just added another 7 years to your loan. Look at loan programs with terms of 15, 20 or 25 years and try to shorten rather then lengthen the remaining term of your loan.

Another term that often comes up during financing is points. Paying points is a way of buying down the interest rate on your loan. Points are actual percentage points. If your loan is for $200,000 and the lender requires you to pay one point, you will have to pay $2,000 to close the deal. Paying one point does not mean that your interest rate will also drop one point. It may only buy down a fraction of a percentage point.

Home Equity Loans

Most banks and other lenders offer home equity loans or lines of credit. This is a way for you to borrow from the equity in your house, using your house to secure the loan. Many lenders encourage you to "pay off those high credit card debts" with this type of loan. From a purely financial perspective, this does make sense. You pay off your credit cards with a low interest loan and you can write off the interest expense. The problem is that this rarely changes a person's spending habits. In fact, most people who do this immediately start spending again. With the additional loan on their house, they are now in danger of jeopardizing their home and the equity they have accumulated.

There is definitely a place for home equity loans. It may be worthwhile or necessary to use this type of loan to pay for repairs or maintenance on your house. But using this type of loan to finance other spending is usually unwise.

Property Taxes, Hazard Insurance and Impound Accounts

In addition to your mortgage payment, you are also required to pay taxes on the property. Property taxes are usually levied by the county in which your house resides. The rate can vary from county to county or state to state but is usually around 1% of the assessed value of the property.

Lenders usually require the house to be covered by hazard insurance. Hazard insurance only covers the value of the house or structure, not the contents. If your home is part of a condominium complex or other type of planned residential development (PRD) where there is a homeowners association, hazard insurance may be covered by the association. Before looking into buying your own policy, check with the association or the association's management company.

Impound Accounts (also referred to as *escrow* accounts) may be required by the lender, especially on loans where the borrower is putting little or no money down. The borrower can also request that an impound account be set up when applying for the loan. An impound account is a type of savings account. Each month the borrower pays an amount in addition to the mortgage payment. This additional amount is deposited into the impound account and withdrawn during the year to pay the property taxes or other expenses. If the lender does not require an impound account on the loan and you elect not to set one up, you then need to set aside money each month to pay your property taxes. Property taxes are usually paid twice a year.

Selling a House

As a seller, if you decide to list your house through a real estate agent, you will be responsible for paying the agent's commission from the proceeds of the sale. Commission rates usually run from 4% to 6% of the final selling price of the house. Both the agent that represents you and the agent that represents the buyer of your house are paid from the proceeds of the sale. In some cases, it will be the same agent, but usually, two agents are involved. The commission will be deducted from the funds you receive at the close of escrow.

In the last 20 years or so, more options have become available for selling your house. Traditional real estate agents still charge a 6% fee to the seller. This fee is split between the selling (or listing) real estate agent/broker and the agent representing the buyer of the house. Some real estate brokers offer a listing fee of 5% in which 2% goes to the listing agent and 3% goes to the buying agent. Some will take that 5% and split it 2.5% to each agent. Brokers such as Help-U-Sell charge various fee levels from approximately 1% to 3.5% depending upon the services selected. The reason that I'm going over these fees in such detail is because realtors can see on their listing sheets the commission they will receive should their client decide to buy your house. Many agents will simply not show homes that do not pay them a fee of 2.5% or higher. I know of one agent that would not show clients any home unless it carried a full 3% commission. It is good to shop around for lower commission rates, but be sure you understand how the commission will be paid to both the listing and the buying agents.

With people using the internet more and more to shop for a variety of products, home sales have now gone on line. Be sure that your listing agent has your home, with pictures, on the internet and that it can be easily accessed by potential buyers.

As with anything, do your homework. Unnecessarily paying an additional 1% to 2% on your home sale could mean $2,000 to $12,000 that goes into your agent's pocket instead of yours.

Investment Property

After building equity in their home, many people start thinking about buying another house or condominium and renting out one of the two as investment property. The idea *sounds* great – someone pays you rent which you then use to pay the mortgage and other expenses on the property. Your renters pay off the mortgage and you still own the house

I know many people who have done well investing in real estate. But, I also know people who have not thoroughly considered the downside of becoming a landlord. In some cases, they almost lost everything.

Three years after buying their house, Bill and Janet check the real estate market and discover their home has increased in value over $50,000. They decide to take $20,000 out of the value of their house by getting a second mortgage. They then take that same money and purchase a condo in the area and find a nice couple to rent the place. The rent does not quite cover the mortgage, taxes, and homeowner dues, but Bill and Janet can easily cover the deficit. At the end of the first year, their tenants move out. During that year, the housing market softened and prices started to fall. There were many vacancies in their area and Bill and Janet had problems finding a new renter. Three months go by and the condo was still vacant. In the mean time, the costs of the condo and their own house ate into their savings. They realized they could no longer continue to support both houses.

There are many endings to this story. The worst is that Bill and Janet are forced to stop making payments on the condo and the bank forecloses on it. Not only would Bill and Janet lose the property, they would also lose the $20,000 they put into it. They would also be required to continue paying on the second mortgage on their own home which they used to finance the $20,000.

Even if Bill and Janet decide to sell the condo, they still need to keep the mortgage current until the property sells. Should the housing market drop suddenly, they may owe more on the house than they can get by selling it.

I am sure that most renters are good people but many can be nightmares. They can cause damage to your property far above the amount of any security deposit you might be holding. If a tenant stops paying rent, it can sometimes take months before you can get them evicted.

Be cautious before buying investment property. Do considerable research. Talk to others who have done the same. As with any investment, do your homework!

An Asset or a Liability?

Just as your house can become one of your best investments, it can also become a liability. We seem to have an obsession to continually "buy up" in the housing market. Americans tend to move every 3 to 5 years and in doing so, lose equity and often incur exorbitant costs along the way.

Let's say Bill and Janet buy their first house for $180,000. Four years later, their house has appreciated in value and they decide to buy something larger. They sell their house for $300,000 and purchase a new home for $375,000.

Here is a list of the costs they incurred in the sale and in improvements to the new house:

Description	Cost
Real Estate Agent Fee	$16,500
Closing Costs	5,500
New Furniture, window coverings, house painting, etc.	10,000
Total	**$32,000**

The cost of selling their house was 5.5% of the 300,000 to the real estate agent and $5,500 for closing costs on both of the houses. After getting settled, they decide that some of their old furniture does not fit well in the new house. They buy new furniture to replace the old and also buy new furniture to fill the additional space. Along with the furniture they buy new window coverings and have the house painted. So far, Bill and Janet have lost $32,000 in equity.

Bill and Janet's monthly costs also increased. They have a larger mortgage payment, the house is bigger so it costs more to heat and cool and their property taxes have increased.

Description	Cost
Additional Mortgage Payment (assuming 6%, 30-year fixed loan)	$520
Electricity, Gas, Water	40
Property Taxes	160
Total Monthly Increase	**$720**

Was the move worth it? Maybe, but Bill and Janet lost $32,000 in equity and increased their monthly expenses by $720. What happens if they make this same type of move every 3 to 5 years? If Bill and Janet stayed in the same house for another six years, and invested the $720 a month they would have spent on the new place (and assuming a 10% return), they would have an investment worth over $70,000. They would also have the $32,000 they lost in equity for a total of just over $100,000.

Do not be fooled into believing that every upgrade you make to your house adds value. You may love hardwood floors and think it is worth the $10,000 you spend, but a potential buyer may love wall-to-wall carpet. The buyer wants you to knock $10,000 off the asking price so they can have the house carpeted. If the housing market is soft and you need to sell, you may be forced to reduce your price.

Try to find a house that will meet your needs for the next 10 years and stay there. Consider the money you spend making improvements and how it will add to the home's value. Like every purchase, everything you want is not everything you need.

Excuse #6: "There is no way I can afford to buy a house." If you are currently renting a two-bedroom apartment, you probably are able to buy a small house or condo. Talk to a real estate agent. Based on your income, he or she can give you a good idea of what you will be able to afford. Talk to a bank or a mortgage broker and find out what kinds of loans will work for you. When you start breaking down the numbers, you will probably find it is possible for you to own your own home. It is one of the best investments you will ever make. When I bought my first condo, I bought a two-bedroom unit and rented out one of the rooms. After taking into consideration the savings on taxes, it actually cost me less to have the condo than it did to rent a one-bedroom apartment.

OK, what do I do now?
- Start planning for your home purchase now.
- Do not wait to buy – take the plunge
- Work closely with your real estate, loan, and escrow agents
- On your home loan, use both a bank (or credit union) and a loan broker to get the best interest rate and to ensure that escrow closes on time.

- If interest rates fall after you purchase your house, look into refinancing at a lower rate.
- Avoid home equity loans for all but necessary maintenance and repairs to your house.
- When selling your home, shop around for different real estate brokers and look closely at their fee structures.
- Be extremely cautious about buying investment property.
- Avoid buying and selling your home every 3 to 5 years. Find a house that meets your needs for the next 10 years and stay there.

Chapter VIII

Your Career - It's Not What You Know, It's Who You Know

The title of this chapter has got to be one of my favorite career excuses of all time. Actually, almost any excuse will do, it does not matter because that is all it is – an excuse. Any time I hear someone complain about why they have not advanced in their career I can usually give at least three good reasons why they have not.

Who you know can be very important in your career. Networking is critical in almost any field. But instead of being used as a motivator, "It's not what you know, it's who you know" is used as an excuse by those resigning themselves to the fate that they have created for their lives.

Your career and your employment are *your* responsibility. No one owes you a job and no one is required to give you a promotion. You will meet people who are prejudiced, biased, or flat out jerks. If you do, find another company and move on. But most people are reasonable. Most managers do want you to move forward and succeed. Give them reasons to hire you and to advance your career – do not give them reasons to leave you behind. If you think that every manager and every company is against you, you are probably the one at fault.

From being on both sides of hiring – the interviewer and the interviewee – I have seen and heard some of the most amazing things. I can only assume at times that some people come in specifically *not* wanting to be hired. Some mistakes are blatant and some are more subtle.

There are excellent books available that go into great detail about writing resumes, writing cover letters, and handling interview questions. In this chapter I want to go into some of the most common errors I have seen on why people do not get hired and why they do not get promoted.

When you look for a job, you immediately enter the sales profession. You are selling yourself and your skills. If you do not start thinking and acting like a salesperson, you are going to be on the short end of the job market. I learned so much working as a financial planner about selling myself and my products that it has benefited me in almost every area of my life.

One of the most important lessons in sales is making a good first impression. It is cliché, but it is also true, "you never get a second chance to make a good first impression." Finding a job and especially finding a good career is a series of making many good first impressions.

Resumes

Your resume is usually your first, "first impression." It is often the only thing your potential employer knows about you. It must be perfect. It has to present the information about you that is applicable to the job for which you are applying and it must show that you are a thorough, thoughtful, able individual. If you have already written a resume, go back and look at it. What does it say about you? If it is filled with misspelled words, poor grammar, or is poorly constructed, it is going to tell the people reviewing it that they do not want to waste their time talking to you.

If you submit your resume to a large company, it is most likely going to go through the human resources department and then be distributed to various other departments. The people in human resources have no idea what type of job is best suited to your skills unless, of course, you tell them on your resume. This has got to be the most common error I see. I read the information and still have no idea what this person does or what type of position he or she is seeking. I am glad that they are "motivated," and that they "learn quickly" but I still need to know what it is they have done and what they want to do now.

When you first start applying for jobs, you have few specific skills on which to draw. So people tend to write generic resumes – throwing in everything they have ever done in their lives and hoping for the best. It is much better to have several versions of your resume and use the one that is most appropriate for the job for which you are applying. I have even written new resumes for one specific job, highlighting the experiences that apply directly to that position. If you are responding to an employment ad, use the same buzz words from the ad in your resume. This makes it far more likely that your resume will get to the right people.

Take extreme care in writing your resume. I know managers who will throw away any resume that has even one misspelled word on it. Why? Because they feel if you cannot take the extra few moments to ensure your resume is correct, you probably will not take the time to make sure your job is done correctly.

An acquaintance I knew borrowed my resume to use as a guide when writing her own. The first paragraph on my resume clearly states what type of job I am seeking. In addition I want the potential employer to know that I have decent writing skills. So I include the following sentence: "... customer liaison experience complemented by excellent verbal and written communication skills." This woman decided to use that same sentence on her resume. When I reviewed what my acquaintance had written I saw the word "complimented" instead of "complemented" in the header. To quote Merriam-Webster, "compliment" is an expression of esteem, respect, affection or admiration. "Complement" is a counterpart or something that completes. She had used the incorrect word. I pointed this out and was told, "Who the hell cares. No one would know that but you." Wrong! Other people do know. I am sure her resume ended up in many wastebaskets.

If you are sending out resumes and not getting interviews, go back and review your resume. Get a book on writing resumes from the library. Restructure it and have other people review it. Resend the new version to the same companies where you sent the old versions. One of the key phrases of sales is "persistence and tenacity." If you are sitting making excuses about life not being fair or that this or that should not matter, you are just saying over and over again "I want to remain in my old position" or "I want to remain unemployed."

Although it is difficult not to become discouraged when your phone is not ringing off the hook for interviews, try to keep in mind that you simply may not be qualified for some of the jobs for which you are applying. There is nothing wrong with aiming high for a better position. There are times when you will be exactly what they are looking for and times that someone is willing to take a chance on you. Be persistent – keep trying, keep looking.

Interviews

The interview is the next important first impression you need to make. It requires the same thoughtfulness and care that you put into your resume. You will have only a short amount of time to sell yourself to your potential employer. The company may be interviewing many people for the position. You have to be the one that they want to hire.

Appearance is critical. Unless you are applying for a job in some trendy industry, you should have a conservative, neat, clean look. Always slightly overdress for the interview. If you are a man it is best to wear a suit and tie or at least dress slacks, a jacket and a tie. Women should also wear a conservative suit or dress. Do not be loud or flashy in your clothing. In John T. Molloy's classic book *Dress for Success* he tells of Charles Revson who founded Revlon Cosmetics. Mr. Revson owned over two hundred suits and every one was conservative navy blue. He knew it was a color that most people found pleasing. Even as the founder and president of a large corporation, Charles Revson knew the importance of always making a good first impression.

I talked to a young man who had interviewed as a bartender at a trendy club. He showed up in a suit and tie for the interview. The club manager asked him why he chose the attire that he did for such a position. He replied, "I wanted to make sure that you remembered me." He got the job.

To me, one of the worst mistakes people make is showing up for an interview smelling strongly of perfume or cologne. Smell is a powerful sense. I absolutely do not want to walk into a conference room and sit there talking to someone for thirty minutes with my nose being assaulted the entire time. All I can think of during the interview is that I want it to come to an end. You may think that you smell wonderful but the person interviewing you may think otherwise. Do not wear cologne or perfume of any kind. It is unlikely it will help you get a job, but it is possible that it might prevent you from getting one.

Pay attention when the person conducting the interview asks questions. Be sure you answer the questions asked. This might seem obvious, but I have been surprised when even a question is repeated, a potential candidate continues to give vague answers. My manager, a co-worker and I interviewed a gentleman for a computer programming position. Early in the interview, my manager asked the man, "How many reports were generated by the last program you worked on?" His reply, "Quite a few."

My manager restated the question, "Just roughly then, was it ten, twenty, one hundred?" Again he replied, "Quite a few." The three of us looked at each other and ended the interview.

Be thorough when answering interview questions but also try to be brief. Try to keep eye contact with the interviewer. Sit up straight in your chair. Lean forward slightly. This body language shows you are interested. Try to avoid negative answers. I do not want to know that your last boss was a jerk. I do not care that your last job was a nightmare. Keep your answers as truthful and positive as possible.

Often at the end of an interview you will be asked, "Do you have any questions?" Be sure to have one or two questions in mind, even if they have been thorough in describing the position and the company. One question I always ask during an interview is "What do you like best about working for this company?" This question usually gets the interviewers talking a little about themselves and starts more of a conversation rather than just someone grilling you for answers.

If you are being interviewed by more than one person at a time, be sure to make eye contact with each one. You need to leave a positive impression on each person in the room.

I worked for a manager who had an amazing track record for hiring good people. What made it even more incredible was that he primarily hired college graduates. Without prior experience on a resume, it is often difficult to decide whether or not to interview and hire a person. I asked him his secret. He said that the first thing he looked for was enthusiasm. He wanted to hire someone who genuinely wanted the job. On your next interview, be sure to show interest in the company and the position – it might make all the difference in the world.

Networking

This brings us back to the title of this chapter, "It's not what you know, it's who you know." That is right. Who you know can be important in getting a job or getting a promotion. Put yourself in a manager's shoes. You need to fill an important position. You have two candidates. Both have excellent qualifications. One you know, having worked together in the past. One you do not know. The candidate you worked with before was a hard worker, got his assignments done on time, and was thorough. Who are you most likely to hire – the known or the unknown quantity?

So, if who you know is so important, then you need to ask yourself how much time do you spend getting to know people? Large companies often have Toastmasters or management clubs you can join. These are excellent avenues to meet other people within your company. Let others know the type of work you do. Find out where they work in the company and what types of positions are available within their departments. Look into professional organizations outside of the company. Go to their meetings. While there, do not just sit at a table and stare at your chips and dip, get up and talk to people. A co-worker attended a training class for a new software design product. During the class he started talking to some of the other students. From the contacts he made that day he got a much better job.

I once attended a seminar on networking. The instructor mentioned job clubs where people out of work meet and receive instruction on resume writing and other skills. Her comment was, "I cannot imagine a worse place to find a job than in a room full of unemployed people." They may provide some good assistance, but you need to get out and meet people that can actually offer you a job. Find out when and where a professional organization in your field meets. Go to the meetings. If it is only for members, ask if you can simply visit for one evening. Talk to people there. Find out what is going on in their companies. Let them know you are looking for a new position.

Even within your own organization or department make sure that people know who you are. A small amount of schmoozing is important for a career. If your manager two or three levels above you knows who you are, what you do, and what you have accomplished, you are more likely to be on the short list when it is time for promotions.

As I said earlier, regardless of your career path, you will always be a salesperson. You constantly need to sell yourself and your skills. Even if you are not looking to climb the corporate ladder, make sure that management knows who you are. This alone can help prevent you from being laid off if your company starts downsizing.

Also, do not burn bridges. Do not leave a company by telling your manager exactly what you think of him or her. You would be surprised at how small of a world it is and how these things can come back to haunt you.

Promotions

Take a good look at your department's or company's organization chart. You will see a few people at the top and many people further down. For every person that takes a step up the corporate ladder, many are left behind. There simply are not enough management positions to promote every person in the company to the top of the chart. What does it take to move up? Who are the people left behind?

A college degree does not necessarily make you smarter, better, harder working, or anything else, but it makes the path to promotions easier. I have heard so many people complain that they missed out on a job or a promotion simply because they did not have a bachelor's or master's degree. They felt they were much better qualified for the position than the person who actually got promoted. That well may be, but a college degree is important and that is unlikely to change. So, you need to go out and get a bachelor's degree if you do not have one or a master's degree if you have already gotten your bachelor's degree. It is going to be difficult and it is going to take time. But if you do not make the time and put forth the effort you are going to find yourself sitting at that same desk you are sitting at now for a long time to come. If the other person was willing to push a little harder and get a degree, maybe that person is the type that will push a little harder at work as well.

If you have been in the same position in the same department or even at the same company for several years, it might be time for you to look for something else. Most people who move up also move around. They look for opportunities in other departments and in other companies. Sometimes they take lateral moves within their own company to get experience in different areas. A driven man I know got his MBA degree and went to work for a large, national company. He took every opportunity available to him to move up. This meant he had to move himself and his family, often across the country, every three to four years. When he felt he had gone as far as possible at that company, he accepted a higher position in another company. He is now the president of a major corporation.

In this electronic age when e-mails are probably the most common form of communication within a company, it is more important than ever to be able to write well. How you write can say volumes about who you are or at least how people perceive you. If your grammar is bad, you constantly misspell words, if you cannot clearly make your point in your e-mails or letters, the recipients tend to see you as "less than" those who do write well. I was fortunate that in my first job I was required to do some technical writing. I worked with two excellent technical writers who gave me outstanding advice on how to write and what common mistakes to avoid. Probably the best book I have read on the subject of non-fiction, technical writing is *On Writing Well* by William K. Zinsser. It is a small book packed full of helpful advice.

Several years ago I held a position in a company that was absolutely fantastic. I liked and respected my boss, my coworkers were sharp and good to work with and the projects were very interesting. I immediately started applying for another job. But not just any job. I started looking for the perfect job and at a much higher salary. Being in such a good position I could take my time to find that "perfect" job. I knew what type of salary I could potentially earn in my industry although I was currently well below that level. I looked, interviewed, ignored insults from placement agencies and two years later found that new position and increased my salary by 55%.

Your attitude is also a big factor in how far you move up in the company. I realize this can mean many different things, but just like in the interview, it seems some people specifically do everything they can to ensure that they do not get promoted. Of course, they will constantly complain and give a myriad of excuses, none of which points back to themselves. Bill worked in a technical company where it was acceptable for employees to wear jeans to work. Management, though, wore more professional attire. He shared an office with a Jeff who was being "fast-tracked" into a management position. But Jeff refused to start dressing the role of a manager. Management even explained that one of the only things delaying the promotion was the way Jeff dressed. His excuse? "That shouldn't matter." In the mean time, Jeff gave many ridiculous excuses as to why he was not promoted. All that was needed was to dress in a more professional manner. I would not be surprised if even much later Jeff changed the way he dressed that the opportunity for a promotion would have already passed by. Management was given too many reasons *not* to promote him. It was not just the way Jeff dressed, it was his attitude that held him back.

Are you working to get work done or are you giving excuses why you cannot accomplish your tasks? Are you comparing yourself to the worst person in the department or the best? This has got to be another of my favorite excuses, "John on the next aisle comes in late every day, why am I penalized when I come in late once in a while?" In the above case of Jeff who did not get promoted because of his attire, I am sure that there was someone, somewhere in the company who was a manager who did not dress professionally. Do not compare yourself to that person, compare yourself to the best and brightest. See what you can do to pull yourself up to their level. Being one step above the worst person in the department is not going to get you very far.

How important is attitude? During the 1970s and 1980s, after the fall of South Vietnam, many Vietnamese people immigrated to the United States looking for opportunities. They came here often not speaking English and from a culture quite different than the one we know. Many came over on small boats with no money and lived in refugee camps when they arrived. They saw the United States as a place of opportunity and their attitudes reflected that. In spite of all the excuses they could give themselves as to why they would not be able to succeed, they succeeded anyway. They faced prejudice and ignored it. They valued education and made sure their children did well in school. They took menial, dead-end jobs when necessary. They saved and invested their money in themselves. They succeeded under circumstances far worse than most U.S.-born Americans will ever have to overcome.

Attitude isn't everything, but with the right attitude almost everything else will fall into place.

Excuse #7: "I'm not taking a dead-end job!" This is one of the most amazing excuses I have heard and I have heard it many, many times. I do not know one successful person that has not held a multitude of dead-end jobs. I worked in a fast food restaurant grilling burgers, at a truck scale weighing trucks and I also delivered office supplies. None of these jobs in and of themselves had any real future. But in each job I gained valuable experience that led me to the next job. Success is measured by both small and big steps. If you are standing still, you just keep standing in the same spot.

OK, what do I do now?

- Make each first impression perfect
- Prepare several versions of your resume – tailor them to specific job opportunities
- Dress conservatively for your interview. Have questions prepared to ask the person conducting the interview.
- Network, network, network
- Improve your writing skills
- Get an advanced degree or additional training
- Attitude can be everything

Chapter IX

Show Me The Value

In this chapter I will discuss more examples of how people make a commitment to poverty. You make that commitment by not looking for value when spending or investing your money. From paying more for items than necessary to being lured into illegal "get rich quick" schemes to investing money in losing propositions, being aware is being prudent.

In the movie "Jerry Maguire," Cuba Gooding Jr.'s character kept demanding someone "Show me the money!" As consumers we need to insist people show us the value of the goods, products and services we purchase.

For every dollar you earn and save there are millions of people in the world who would like to take that dollar away from you. Most will try to take it from you legally and some will try to take it from you illegally. But legal separation from your money does not mean the recipient is acting ethically nor does it mean you have spent or invested wisely.

Many people believe that "you get what you pay for." If I sold you a can of soda for $20 does that mean it is worth $20? What if I bought that same can at a store for fifty cents, put a new label on it and sold it for $5. Would you think it was any better than the original? Sadly, many consumers think this is true.

Obviously, you do need to pay for quality. The lowest priced items are rarely the best. In looking for value, in no way am I suggesting you should simply look for the cheapest price. You need to weigh the price against the quality. At some point though, as the price of a product rises, the increase in the quality either does not change or changes very little.

I was in Las Vegas and realized I had forgotten to bring a neck tie with me. There was a large mall connected to the hotel where I was staying. I walked into a men's shop, was approached by a salesman and began looking at their selection of ties. I found one I liked and turned it over to check the price. It was $450!! Maybe, and I do mean *maybe*, there was about $10 worth of tie that I held in my hand. So where was the other $440? It was in the label, in the store with the nice fixtures and especially in their hopes that I honestly thought that I was getting $450 worth of a tie. Sorry – I did not see $450 worth of value so I did not buy it.

Many items, such as sunglasses, are manufactured by only a handful of companies in the world. These companies come up with a myriad of designs and then show them to famous fashion houses. The companies select the sunglass designs that interest them, add their labels and resell them to the public. The glasses they buy for $5 are resold for $200 after their labels are attached. The same designs may be sold to other companies as well – the same $5 glasses but with different labels. Some will sell for $200 some will sell for only $20.

One of the most common items in a man's wardrobe is the cotton polo shirt. There are different weights of cotton fabric, construction and fit, but just because a designer logo is sewn onto the front does not mean that a $20 shirt suddenly becomes a $180 shirt. If you believe that it does, you are not looking for value nor are you spending wisely.

Decide which is more important to you – having the appearance of wealth or actually being wealthy. Financial independence allows you to enjoy the comfort and security that comes with that wealth. Is trying to impress people that you don't even know really all that important?

Pyramid or Ponzi Schemes

Pyramid schemes are illegal, yet every few years they re-emerge with new packaging. Each time they draw in a new congregation of believers who ultimately end up losing their money. Some do profit but they are the ones at the top of the pyramid.

Pyramid schemes work much like chain letters. You enter the pyramid at the bottom, giving money to the person at the top. For you to move up the pyramid, you must bring 5 or so additional people into the scheme. When your name gets to the top of the pyramid, you get the money from the people entering at the bottom.

As long as there are people to feed into the pyramid, it keeps working. But once interest wanes, everyone in the middle of the pyramid ends up with nothing after they have already given their money to the person at the top. Some high-flying pyramid schemes require people at the bottom to give $1,000 to the person at the top. If there are five levels to the pyramid and each person is required to bring in an additional five people, by the time your name gets to the top you will receive about $180,000. Doesn't that sound just too good to be true? Of course it does. When pyramid schemes start they tend to spread like wildfire and then die just as quickly. That, or the police show up and everyone involved gets arrested.

Mail Fraud and Other Scams

There are thousands of ways you can be separated from your money via scams. Each day, new scams appear and find new victims. Scams called "advance fee" are some of the most prevalent. The one thing they have in common is that you are promised large sums of money by helping someone bring cash into the country, helping them invest money, or one of many other stories. Somewhere along the line, you will be required to put up some of your own money to bribe, advance, establish an account, or one of many other excuses. Once you do that, it will be the last time you see your money as well as the last time you will see or hear from the person conducting the scam. There are mail fraud scams where people are told they have won a new car or other big-ticket item and all they need to do is pay for the shipping. Of course, shipping a car is expensive. So, you need to send them $500 to cover the costs. After sending the $500 you will not hear from them again, you will never get the car and you will never see your money again.

Scam artists often prey on the elderly. Keep a close watch on your parents or grandparents so that they do not become victims of these crooks. My own grandmother was ripe for the picking by these scumbags and her name and address must have been circulated on some sort of grifter's mailing list. Once we became aware that she had been sending money to several questionable companies, we had to intercept her mail and go through it before giving it to her. No matter how many times we told her that these were scams and not to send any of them money, her hope that she had somehow hit it big would get the best of her. We have no idea how much money was lost before we found out.

Multi-Level Marketing (MLM)

Multi-level marketing companies are perfectly legal. Although they look much like pyramid schemes to me, they insist they are not and continue to operate throughout the United States.

Multi-level marketing is an approach to selling products and services whereby the salesperson usually works independently from the company which provides the products. The salesperson is paid commissions based on the amount of products or services he or she sells. They also recruit new salespeople and receive a portion of their commissions as well. As each salesperson under him or her recruits new salespeople, a smaller and smaller portion of the commission works its way up to the multiple levels of "managers." Usually, when new salespeople are recruited, they are required to pay some sort of fee, often explained as a type of franchise fee. This fee is often several hundred dollars and like the commissions, finds its way up the chain of "managers" and is divided among them.

New recruits are invited to a meeting with a vague invitation that usually reads as follows: "My thirty-four year old brother has just started a new business. He is doing so well that he would like to tell you about it. He is planning on retiring in two years and needs motivated, entrepreneurial people to take it over. He is having a small gathering of people at his house to discuss this exciting opportunity." If you ask questions about exactly what type of business this is, you will be told that it will all be explained in the presentation. During the presentation you will be told of doctors and lawyers who have abandoned their practices because they are making so much money with this business opportunity. You will be shown how if you recruit just two new salespeople a month that within a year you will be making a six-figure income. But the opportunity and the reality are usually far, far apart.

I have never been involved with an MLM company, but I have been recruited and attended a couple of presentations. Each time I was assured this one was different, that it did not have the same pitfalls as prior MLMs. Each time, I found the same gimmicks and problems.

79

A friend was recruited to attend a meeting of a new MLM. The meeting was near my home so he asked if I would go with him. Through this MLM, the salesperson would buy internet "malls" from the company. These malls would be portals to large department stores and other name brand product websites. Each time a person entered the salesperson's mall and purchased a product, the salesperson or "mall owner" would receive a commission. This idea did have some merit in that people would be buying products they already did use. You would not be trying to sell them highly priced soap or nutritional products they may or may not want. The salesperson would buy these malls from the company and resell them to new mall owners below him or her. Each mall sold for about $300. During the presentation they encouraged each person to get started in the company by buying ten malls and then reselling them. They showed over and over again the buckets of money you would make as each person tells two friends and sells mall after mall after mall.

After the presentation we were pulled into an office where three people hammered on us to sign up. Again they described all of the money we would make as more and more recruits bought these malls. I just sat there silent. Finally, because I was not saying anything, they asked me what I thought. Didn't I understand the opportunity? Didn't I understand how I would be making lots of money? I finally told them that the one thing they never mentioned was how much in sales of product, not malls they were making. All they talked about was selling these malls that had no value whatsoever and that this money was just being passed up the chain. To me, that is a pyramid scheme, nothing more.

The people who had formed the company were making lots and lots of money, though. They got a cut of every single mall sold. They were not overly interested in the sales of products, there was just way too much money in the "mall business."

I am sure that somewhere out there, there is someone who has honestly done well in an MLM and who was not one of the original founders. Speaking of that, do not be fooled by being told that you are getting in on the "ground floor." By the time the average person hears about a new MLM, the top of the pyramid has already formed. I have never known anyone who has gotten involved in one of these that did not ultimately feel that they had wasted their money and their time. Some also got stuck with a garage full of products they had been required to purchase when they became a "distributor."

Timeshare Condominiums and Vacation Clubs

Timeshares and vacation clubs are the ultimate "show me the value" operations of all time. I have looked and looked for the value and have yet to find it. I have attended the presentations, listened to the promises, been told by friends what "great investments" these are and still I am unimpressed.

Never, never make any major decision, whether it be financial or emotional when your head is not in a calm, sane place. If you are upset, do not tell off your boss and walk off your job. Go home and cool off. If you are shown a financial opportunity and someone has just spent thirty minutes pumping you up, getting you excited and then telling you that you have to sign up right now or the opportunity will pass you by, *let it pass you by.* Something is wrong, possibly very wrong.

The basic concept of a timeshare condominium is that a developer builds a complex, usually in some sort of resort area. They then take each condo unit, divide the selling price by 52 (for the 52 weeks in a year) and sell each week to the public. The owner of that week can use the condo each year for the week purchased. Some weeks cost more than other weeks just as some units cost more than others. If you absolutely love going to Hawaii or some other vacation spot each year at exactly the same time, this may sound like a good deal.

The first place where I do not see the value in timeshares is with the initial purchase price. If you take the price of the one week you purchase and multiply it by 52 you would think it would come out to be approximately the price of buying an entire condo in the same area. This is where you would be wrong. The price is marked up anywhere from 2 to 5 times the market rate for a similar condo. Many years ago my parents owned a condo in Hawaii. It was a small oceanfront studio unit. They eventually sold it for about $110,000. At that same time, timeshare condos were being sold in the same area. One week for a studio unit was selling for $10,000. If you multiply $10,000 by 52 weeks you get $520,000! That is almost five times the price of my parent's unit. So what did you actually buy? One fifty-second of my parent's condo would sell for about $2,100. What happened to the other $8,000? It all went to commissions and profits for the salespeople and the developers. On top of the $10,000, the new owner was required to pay annual maintenance fees, property taxes, usage fees, and should they trade their week for a week at another condo, they would also be required to pay transfer fees. When these people went to sell their interest in their timeshare, they found that there were no buyers. Too many other people wanted out of their commitment and no one was around to hard sell the concept. Instead of getting their original $10,000 investment, many were lucky to get anything back. Those that did often got pennies on the dollar.

As people began to catch on that timeshare condos were not all that attractive an investment, developers needed a way to re-package them. There was far too much money to be made in this industry for them to just roll over and retire. This is when vacation clubs were born.

I recently went to a presentation for a popular vacation club in my area and took notes. The presentation was held at the business offices of the marketing arm of the vacation club. The facilities took up an entire half floor of a large high-rise office building. I was led into a large meeting room to wait for the formal presentation. While waiting, we were shown a slide show of the many properties owned by this vacation club. The rooms shown from each property were always spacious one or two bedroom condominiums with balconies overlooking the ocean or other beautiful vistas. People were enjoying themselves skiing down snow laden slopes, playing in the water, jet skiing on a lake or on the ocean, or families simply playing games by the fire in their beautiful condo. All the condos were clean, large and beautiful.

After a while a representative came in to explain the opportunity. She explained a little of the background of the company, how it was formed and that one of the primary objectives was to provide a vacation club and vacation destinations that were "Really high quality, really low cost, and inflation proof." This company owns many properties throughout the United States. With this club, you pay a one-time fee and each year "vacation dollars" are deposited into your account. With these dollars, you can purchase time in any one of many vacation resorts. She said that with these vacation dollars you could spend time in anything from a one-room studio up to a penthouse suite.

She continued by saying that you can also go outside their network and stay at properties all over the world. She gave an example of a family from a prior presentation that was to visit Disney World. They had made reservations at a luxury resort costing $529 a night. The family felt this vacation club was such a great bargain that they signed up the same night.

If you stay outside of their network, the transfer fees were only $121 for a domestic hotel and $149 for an international hotel. She told of a trip she had recently taken to Scotland where she stayed in a castle. The cost? Well, only $149 for the entire week!

After the presentation we were individually called out of the room by sales representatives and taken to another area of the office complex. My sales rep, Adam called me out of the room and I followed him to his sales desk. I told Adam that I usually take two weeks of vacation a year and I wanted to know how many "vacation dollars" I needed to purchase to make this happen. I also wanted to know the cost. It appeared that the basic buy in amount was for 6,000 vacation dollars a year at a one-time cost of $9,300. The $9,300 could be financed by the company by putting 10% down and the remainder would be carried by the company for seven years at 13.9% interest. In other words, I would need to write a check (or charge the amount) for $930 and then make a payment of $156.39 a month for the next seven years. On top of that amount, I would be required to pay $357 a year (or $89.25 a quarter) in maintenance fees, taxes, and insurance. After further questioning, he admitted this fee could increase from year to year.

Adam asked me several times how much I had paid for my last vacation. I am not sure how this was a valid question because all I would get out of the vacation club was my lodging. A more reasonable question would have been "how much did you spend per night for a hotel on your last vacation?"

Adam showed me a catalog of the various properties owned by the club. I wanted to see what type of accommodations my annual 6,000 vacation dollars would buy for a two-week vacation. Fortunately, I asked to review the catalog myself and looked more closely at the costs. What he had said earlier about 6,000 vacation dollars buying an annual two-week vacation was not *exactly* true.

Ok, let's start breaking this down. Let's go through the sales pitch and the current and future costs of signing up for this club. For my example, I am using one of their properties in Hawaii. A one-week stay in a studio condo costs 8,000 vacation dollars. Wait a minute!! Adam told me I could get two weeks for only 6,000 vacation dollars. Well, that is true but only under the most ideal circumstances and only at certain properties. So, this means that in the first year I will not have enough vacation dollars to take my trip. But – not a problem – I can roll over my vacation dollars into the next year. So, in the second year I will have enough vacation dollars to take my one-week trip. But, it will not be in the big, beautiful two-bedroom condo I saw on the video, it will be in a one-room studio that is much like a hotel room. I can get that two-bedroom unit but it will cost me 12,000 vacation dollars.

I checked on the internet for comparable properties in the same area as their resort and found a studio unit for $125 a night or $875 for the entire week. With this information, let's compare over a seven-year period, which is the length of the financing, what we will get through the vacation club and what we could have if we create our own investment vacation fund for the same amount of money.

Over the seven-year period, accumulating 6,000 vacation dollars a year, our vacation club owner could take five, one-week vacations to Hawaii. Each year he will pay $1,877 in total monthly payments and $357 in maintenance fees for a total of $2,234. The first year he will also pay the down payment of $930 for a total that year of $3,164.

In our own investment vacation fund, we will spend the same amount each year as the vacation club owner. We will take the same number of trips to Hawaii in a comparable condo unit. Out of the annual costs, we will pay for our hotel room and the balance of the money we will invest in a mutual fund. For the investment I am assuming an average annual return of 8% and calculating it on a monthly basis.

	Vacation Club		Investment Vacation Fund			
Year-Vacation?	Cost		Hotel Cost	Amt Invested	Total	Value of Investment Fund
1-No	**$3,164**		$0	$3,164	**$3,164**	$3,325
2-Yes	**2,234**		875	1,359	**2,234**	5,919
3-Yes	**2,234**		875	1,359	**2,234**	8,728
4-Yes	**2,234**		875	1,359	**2,234**	11,770
5-No	**2,234**		0	2,234	**2,234**	15,065
6-Yes	**2,234**		875	1,359	**2,234**	17,725
7-Yes	**2,234**		875	1,359	**2,234**	20,606
TOTAL	**$16,568**		**$4,375**	**$12,193**	**$16,568**	**$20,606**

At the end of seven years, the vacation club owner will have paid $16,568 and taken five, one-week trips to Hawaii and stayed in a one-room studio condo. The investment vacation fund owner will have also paid $16,568 and also taken five, one-week trips to Hawaii and stayed in a one-room studio condo. The vacation club owner has paid off his obligation. The investment vacation fund owner has an investment account worth $20,606.

Ok, I am already ahead of you here. Of course, after the seventh year, the vacation club owner's costs drop off dramatically. But, he is still required to pay the annual maintenance fee of $357. So, based on the sales pitch, this is where the vacation club should begin to pay off. Right? Well, if our investor now takes his $20,606 and amortizes it over the next 20 years earning an average rate of 5%, he will receive $1,632 a year to help pay for vacations. So, the vacation club owner continues to *pay* $357 a year and the personal investment vacation fund owner *receives* $1,632 a year for the next twenty years. Also, the investment vacation fund owner can choose any destination and any hotel in the world for his vacation, he is not limited to properties within any one network.

To put it a little more simply and not using any sort of investment fund, over a 20-year period, the vacation club owner will pay $21,209 into the club and will be able to take 15 trips to Hawaii. For that same amount of money, the non-vacation club owner can take 20 trips to Hawaii and still have $3,709 left over.

Here are some other problems I have with the vacation club:

1. When I checked for availability at the condo in Hawaii for the following year, any one of the four months I checked was already completely booked. I was looking anywhere from 8 to 12 months in the future and nothing was available. With my own vacation plan, I have thousands of rooms to choose from, I am not limited to any one or two resorts.

2. Hotels in Europe available through the club were usually located miles outside of the cities. In Paris, it would be a 45-minute train ride from the resort into the center of Paris. In Rome, you would need to rent a car to drive the one-hour trip each way. Not only does the resort isolate you from the city, much of your precious vacation time is wasted traveling to and from the resort.

3. In the above Disney World example, the sales rep mentioned a luxury resort at a cost of $529 a night. If you book a vacation through the club, you are likely to stay at a modest, well-known hotel chain. A friend of mine just went to Orlando, stayed at this same hotel and the room cost $79 a night. With the vacation club, you might also have to pay the $121 out-of-network fee. This sales representative was comparing a $3,700 a week hotel to one that would cost only $553 a week if you booked it directly.

4. You are told you are an owner in the club and that this ownership can be sold or passed on to your children or other friend or family member. There does not appear to be any limit to the number of memberships that can be sold in this club. Each membership sold dilutes the ownership value of all the previous owners. If this was actually worth $9,300, you should be able to sell it for $9,300 or even more over time. The reality is that you will probably find your membership difficult to sell. If you cannot sell it, it has no real value.

5. I recently discovered that the company now charges occupancy taxes and housekeeping fees. These fees add $125 to the cost of a one-week vacation. Unlike what was stated in the presentation, the club does not seem to be "inflation proof."

6. The vacation club marketing company calls regularly and offers upgrades to your vacation account. By financing an additional $2,000 or $3,000 you could add 2,000 or more vacation dollars to your account every year. I know of one woman who has constantly upgraded and in doing so has been paying on her membership for the last 12 years. Also, every time you increase the amount of your annual credits, it also increases the amount you pay on annual maintenance fees.

7. Sales of timeshare condos are limited to the 52 weeks in a year. If you own a week in the condo, you are guaranteed your vacation time. Many vacation clubs have no such limits. They can sell unlimited memberships. This means that if everyone in the club decides to take a vacation in the same year, there simply may not be rooms available for each club member.

Lastly, if you still think this type of club has tremendous value and is worth every cent of the $9,300 you will pay, think again. Just like timeshare condos, these clubs are sold using high-pressure tactics for a reason. If you go onto the internet, you will find people trying to get out of their memberships and are willing to sell them for far less than what you will pay the night of the presentation. Many offer vacation dollars already banked and balances half the original purchase price.

When I told Adam that I needed to think about the opportunity, he told me the $9,300 price included a one-time $3,500 discount. I would only get this discount if I signed up that same night. If you ever hear something like this during a sales presentation, it should immediately alert you that something is wrong. Stand up and leave and research it further. In the case of this vacation club, Adam obviously did not want me to learn that I could find the same thing cheaper on an internet website.

Excuse #8: "I'm happy with my purchase and that's all that matters."
Unfortunately, this is how most people feel. If you are not interested in spending your money wisely and you do not look for value in what you do buy, you are also making a very serious commitment to poverty.

OK, what do I do now?
- Shop for value. Highest prices rarely mean highest quality or best value.
- If something sounds too good to be true, it probably is
- Never pay for the "privilege" to sell someone's product.
- If someone tries to sell you something with the line "this price is for today only," walk away. They are probably trying to take advantage of you
- Avoid time share condos and vacation clubs.

Chapter X

Living Paycheck To Paycheck: Whose Fault Is It Anyway?

In the late 1990s and in the year 2000, the stock market rallied to levels never seen before. The market behaved completely irrationally. Investors threw money into dot com companies that had no possibility of making profits within the first five to ten years. Even supposed financial analysts on television talked of the "new economy," and that maybe profits and p/e (price/earning) ratios didn't mean much anymore. With that, all the ducks were lined up to indicate the stock market was near a top and the economy was beginning to head south.

As people cashed out their profits in the stock market, this led to tax revenues that many states, especially California, had never seen before. Like children in a candy store, the California state legislature and the governor spent as if this well of money would not run dry. When revenues increased 25%, they responded by increasing spending by 40%. When the economy began to slow and California's budget surplus quickly turned into a deficit, the finger pointing began.

One top state official said, "No one could have seen this coming. No one could have known that the economy would slow down or that tax revenues would decline." No one? Anyone over the age of twenty should remember the slow down in the economy in the late 1980s. Anyone older than that remembers the recession of the 1970s. Economies rise and fall. Anyone believing otherwise is a fool.

The biggest trap people get into is spending more than they earn. Credit cards make this so simple that we think nothing of it. "Everyone is doing it, so what's the big deal?" Yes, even our elected officials are just that naïve or more likely, just stupid. Within your lifetime, regardless of how prosperous you become, you will experience times that are good and times that are not so good. Assuming that only good times are ahead is how we keep from attaining financial independence and instead live paycheck to paycheck.

I worked for a department in a large company that hired many people right out of college. As with most college students, they were accustomed to living on almost nothing. Suddenly, they thought they were earning big bucks and immediately started spending it all. They bought cars they could not afford, joined gyms, and bought clothes from Nordstrom. The banks saw new potential credit card addicts and were only too happy to extend more and more credit. Within a short time, these people created huge barriers to reaching financial freedom as well as often limiting their career opportunities.

It is not unusual to change jobs or careers several times during our lives. At times, taking two or three steps forward means first taking one step back. I have known people trapped in jobs they hate because advancing would mean first taking that step backward. By backwards, I mean a cut in pay. They are living "paycheck to paycheck" and cannot afford to live on less money. They have wedged themselves into a corner and now cannot improve their lives.

As a broker, asking questions about a customer's financial situation, it never seemed to matter how much they made. If the pattern was set early of living on the financial edge, the problem persisted. If they made $30,000 they saw financial nirvana at $50,000. Yet when they earned $60,000, they were still mired in credit card debt that continued to increase along with their income. If they believed they could not cut their spending and invest part of their income during the good times, how were they going to be able to survive when times turned bad?

The test of credit trouble is simple – if you are charging items and are unable to pay the balance at the end of the month, you are mis-using credit.

Throughout this book I have often talked about borrowing money and the pitfalls to avoid. There are times in your life when debt and credit are important. Paying cash for a house or a car is pretty much out of the reach of most Americans. We must borrow to purchase these items. Buying a house is one of the few good reasons to assume debt. But even that can get you into trouble if you stretch yourself too thin.

Establishing credit is important and having a credit card in today's world is pretty much a necessity. But once we get that little piece of plastic in our hands, our shopping impulses kick in and that $2,000 or $5,000 credit limit gets quickly eaten up. Right away we owe a substantial part of our annual income and we are paying outrageously high interest rates on that money.

Soon, we owe more than we can handle. At this point, people think they can just skip a monthly payment because, after all, "it's just a department store credit card." Regardless of the type of card, all credit activity is recorded with three major credit reporting companies. Once you start missing payments you start damaging your credit. Later, when you decide to buy a car or a house, you may have to pay higher interest rates or you may be unable to get a loan at all.

I gave an example in an earlier chapter of buying a big screen television and financing the purchase. That was merely an *example*. Do not do that in your own life. If you want the big screen TV and you cannot pay for it in cash, *do not buy it*. You cannot afford it. Start saving your money and buy what you can afford, but buy it with cash. If you do charge it make sure you can pay off the balance when you receive your bill.

At the end of each chapter I gave excuses why people do not reach their financial goals. The most imaginative excuses I have ever heard always seem to apply to why people have gotten themselves deeply into debt. Probably my all time favorite reads something like this "There was this fantastic sale at Macy's and I saved $200 on this new outfit!" You didn't save anything. If the outfit ended up costing $250 after the mark down, you *spent* $250. If the $250 was charged, you are now $250 deeper in debt plus the interest you are likely to pay as well. Oh, and yes, you do have a new outfit.

The fact that something is on sale does not justify increasing your debt. If you have the cash, if you are truly in need of new clothing, if you find a sale, and if the cost of the clothing is within your budget, then by all means buy it. But a perceived "good deal" does not justify any impulse purchase on credit.

When I worked as a broker I met this nice couple. I drove to their home and arrived at a modest but lovely home in the country surrounded by several acres of land. When I started getting in to their financial position, I discovered they were worth well over $20 million. There were no luxury cars in the driveway, no designer label clothing, no servants waiting on their every need. In fact, the husband was building shelves in the kitchen for his wife. These people were not lawyers or doctors. They were your average next door neighbor who worked hard during their lives, saved, invested their money and became wealthy. They did not indulge their every whim. They bought what they needed, treated themselves at times to what they enjoyed and now had no financial worries.

Our society loves to disparage Bill Gates for all of his billions yet we worship celebrities in the entertainment industry and their excessive indulgence. The boxer, Mike Tyson recently filed for bankruptcy. This is someone who made over $300 million in his career and still spent more than he earned. The stories of actors, singers and athletes becoming rich and later filing bankruptcy have become far too common. Why is Bill Gates the bad guy? Bill Gates' company employs thousands of people. Microsoft stock has made fortunes for millions of its stock holders. The bad guys are those that squander what they earn, make no plans for the future, and assume that nothing bad can ever happen to them.

One of the most common truths I found as a broker is that no matter what we earn, it is never enough. We tend to live beyond our income. Someone making $50,000 a year cannot possibly save anything because of the high cost of living. That same argument is made by a person earning $100,000 or even $200,000 a year. They are all living paycheck to paycheck. Our government officials even provide us with excuses as to why it isn't our fault. It *is* our fault. We are the most prosperous nation in the world. We have a living standard beyond what people in most countries can even imagine. And yet, we spend our lives into debt rather than taking a small portion of our income and setting it aside to secure our future and possibly the future of our children.

There are people who desperately need to buy a house but their finances are stretched so thin that they cannot come up with the money they need to get the ball rolling. These are not people making $15,000 or $20,000 a year. These are people making $60,000 to $100,000. What a total waste of an opportunity.

If you are living paycheck to paycheck you need to immediately look at your life and start cutting back. Just because something "only costs $20 a month" does not mean you need it or should have it. A cell phone, cable TV, a high-speed internet connection, a new car every two to three years are all things that are not necessities. Jack was on welfare with two children. Bill, Jacks' brother, went to his place only to find that Jeff had cable TV with premium channels. Bill immediately called the cable company and cancelled. Jeff's response? "I *have* to have cable TV!" Believe it or not there was actually a time when there was no cable TV and even more shocking, a time when there wasn't even television and yet people still found ways to be entertained.

We are fascinated by the thought of being "millionaires" thinking if we only had a million dollars our lives would be perfect. Lottery winners often start buying lavishly only to soon find that their money has run out and they are once again broke. A million dollars invested wisely can provide financial security, but only if you are cautious. Twenty years ago you could find a safe investment paying 8% and you could live off of that million dollars earning $80,000 a year. Now bank certificate of deposits are paying only 1.2%. That drops your annual income down to only $12,000 a year. Your million dollars suddenly is not going as far as you first thought. If you start drawing against the principal, you will have less and less each year.

As I have said before, financial independence is available to almost every working American, but it takes discipline, a conservative fiscal attitude and tenacity. It means not indulging in every whim. It means financial planning instead of careless spending. It means learning a little about the financial markets and making wise, conservative investments. It means not viewing every possession as some sort of right or something that you deserve. It means taking responsibility for your choices. It does not have to mean always living without, but it does mean that you can't always get exactly what you want exactly when you want it.

Start today. As I said in Chapter III, begin by setting aside 2% of your income into an investment program. Each time you get a raise, up the amount by another 2%. If you have a lot of credit cards, get rid of most of them. Keep one or two major cards but put them away, pay them off and do not carry them with you. You will be amazed at the end of the first year just how far you have come. At the end of five years, you will be even more surprised. Most people do not become wealthy overnight. It takes time and planning. Now it is your turn.

Excuse # Whatever: Stop making excuses. Stop being a victim. Stop envying what others have. Stop making a commitment to poverty. Just go and make it happen for you and your family.

OK, what do I do now?
- Create a budget and live within your means
- Avoid credit card debt
- Take responsibility for your choices in life
- Start long and medium term investment programs
- Stop making excuses

Printed in the United States
202716BV00004B/163-168/A